JEANNE SCHNITZLER is Associate Professor of Design
at the California State University at Los Angeles.
GINNY ROSS is Needlework Product Manager
for Hazel Pearson Handicrafts, Inc.,
Rosemead, California.

BOOKS IN THE CREATIVE HANDCRAFTS SERIES

THE CREATIVE HANDCRAFTS SERIES

New Dimensions In Needlework

JEANNE SCHNITZLER / GINNY ROSS

A SPECTRUM BOOK

PRENTICE-HALL, INC., ENGLEWOOD CLIFFS, NEW JERSEY 07632

Library of Congress Cataloging in Publication Data

Schnitzler, Jeanne.
  New dimensions in needlework.

  (The Creative handcrafts series) (A Spectrum Book)
  Includes index.
    1. Canvas embroidery.   I. Ross, Ginny, joint author.
II. Title.
TT778.C3S32   746.4′4   76-26016
ISBN 0-13-612622-7
ISBN 0-13-612614-6 pbk.

A Spectrum Book

10 9 8 7 6 5 4 3 2 1

Printed in the United States of America

PRENTICE-HALL INTERNATIONAL, INC., *London*
PRENTICE-HALL OF AUSTRALIA PTY. LIMITED, *Sydney*
PRENTICE-HALL OF CANADA, LTD., *Toronto*
PRENTICE-HALL OF INDIA PRIVATE LIMITED, *New Delhi*
PRENTICE-HALL OF JAPAN, INC., *Tokyo*
PRENTICE-HALL OF SOUTHEAST ASIA PTE. LTD., *Singapore*
WHITEHALL BOOKS LIMITED, *Wellington, New Zealand*

Contents

v

vi

Preface

The marvelous potential of needle and threads has held endless fascination for mankind since the dawn of history. Although needlework was originally conceived to serve utilitarian demands, the inventive genius of the human mind was quick to endow the products of the needle with such expressive qualities that it soon achieved status beyond that of simply a craft and gained renown as a treasured, dignified, and enduring art form.

In its broadest interpretation, the term *needlework* encompasses a wide variety of techniques and applications. *New Dimensions in Needlework* places specific focus on those design concepts, techniques, and materials that relate directly to the form of needlework commonly referred to as *needlepoint.* Major emphasis has been given to concepts and techniques that offer new-found freedom to anyone desiring to design his or her own style of needlepoint. A broad scope has been developed to reach needle-pointers on all working levels, from the amature hobbyist to the professional craftsman.

Chapters 2 through 6 explore and examine the elements and principles of design that are the basic tools of artistic expression. In addition, ideas for design and design sources are cited to encourage a highly individual approach to and analysis of creative endeavor. Much of the content is developed through visual presentations, which are both more appropriate and better related to a graphic art than are verbal ones.

In every valid form of art-craft the essential components are craftsmanship, technique, and creative interpretation. A total design concept cannot be achieved until these three factors are brought together in perfect union. Chapters 7 through 10 present clear and concise directions for developing the basic know-how of needlework techniques. In this section the beginning needlepointer will find step-by-step procedures to aid in every phase of needlepoint, from threading a needle and selecting canvas and yarn, to the necessary final steps for finishing a well-executed project.

Graphs designed for quick and easy interpretation are presented to set up the foundation for a needlework vocabulary featuring the five basic stitches. Following these are thirty-five additional stitch variations from which to expand.

Experienced needlepointers will find in this volume information and insights into random techniques seldom considered either in or out of print. How to blend dye lots and identify the canvas nap when the selvage has been removed are but two of the helpful hints that can assist in perfecting expertise. Inspiration may well be drawn from the compendium of stitches, offered which includes a contemporary approach to the ancient art of pulled yarn.

No attempt has been made to define the ultimate dimensions that can be reached in this ever-expanding art form; there are, however, many fine examples in this book of exceptional pieces of contemporary needlework. Modern-day needlework designers from across the United States and Great Britain have enthusiastically contributed works revealing the exciting new directions and techniques that are the products of the essence of an old art finding new meaning in terms of today.

The greatest gift of the twentieth century is the realization that all knowledge is expandable. To those who do indeed seek new dimensions in needlework, the pages of this book are dedicated.

Acknowledgements

One of the great joys in assembling any publication grows out of the contacts and relationships established with the many people who so graciously devote their time, effort, and interest to the project at hand. Most sincere appreciation is extended to:

Frederick Mollern, whose selective eye and sensitive photographs in the chapters on Design, Texture, Color History and can You Find the Dimensions of a Square, not only enrich the printed word but also make their own unique contribution to the essence of needlepoint design. His exceptional kindness and understanding turned many hours of work into a pleasant adventure.

Susan Thomas Babb, Assistant Curator of Costume and Textiles, Los Angeles County Museum of Art, whose patience and expertise were invaluable in securing information and pictures for the historical content. Her warm friendship and assistance lent welcome support both mentally and physically.

Mary Gormley, Librarian, California State University at Los Angeles, for her help, enthusiasm and persistant determination in searching out elusive volumes from both here and abroad.

The many designers, craftsman and scholars who so graciously responded by contributing work, photographs, letters and information to be included in this work.

xi

Acknowledg-ments

Michael Hunter, Director of Spectrum Books, whose wise and steady counsel aided greatly in the preparation and organization of this undertaking.

Erich, whose interest, support and ''helpfulness'' never faltered in spite of his tender years.

J.S.

To all my creative friends in the professional world of needlepoint, I say ''Thank you—your tremendous talents are unsurpassed.'' A special thanks to Sherry Baker, National Needlework News, for her assistance. To all my wonderful friends who willingly assisted in the stitching of so many projects, I say, ''Thank you for a job well done—you have made this book a dream come true.''

G.R.

"Exploration of Light, Space and Plane" by Jeanne Schnitzler
is a monocoque structure composed of a monofilament ground
suspended in lucite. Mylar, twisted cellophane, nylon,
and plastic combine to create an interplay of translucent forms
structured alternately in needlework stitches and weaving.

1 The Joys of Needlework

INTRODUCTION

Common but not commonplace, the needle is a simple tool at best. Over the centuries it has changed little in either form or function and the essence of its vitality remains inexorably bound to hand and mind.

The rebirth taking place in every area of the textile arts has stimulated renewed interest in needlework. Traditional methods of decorative stitching continue to expand and develop through exploration, advanced technology, and creative innovation, which in turn have gained increased momentum from popular appeal. *New Dimensions in Needlework* penetrates the broad spectrum of needlework to concentrate on that one method known as needlepoint.

Needlepoint is deeply rooted in ancient methods of both weaving and embroidery. As in weaving, its ground and structure are interdependent and undergo modification simultaneous to the introduction of pattern. As an extension of embroidery, needlepoint employs a technique composed entirely of stitches which are often identical in nature to those used by the embroiderer. Differences between the two occur from the fact that embroidery stitches are not subject to the inherent direction and weave of the ground for their form, nor are they used to complete ground structure. Needlepoint, on the other hand, derives its identifying characteristic from the application of threads to the open grid of a given ground. Form results when ground and threads unite to support and perpetuate one another. This means that all methods used to create design and structure must be compatible with the established limitations of a predetermined grid.

Needlepoint has many advantages over other techniques used to create decorative textiles. One of the most obvious advantages is that each stitch can be controlled as design elements build, allowing for change or variation as taste dictates. The wide selection of materials available to modern day needlepointers accommodates great variety in design form. There are materials for developing intricate subjects, refined shading techniques, and delicate details. Those desiring a bolder approach will find both coarse and heavy canvases which encourage the use of a novel selection of yarns and stitches.

Participation in needlepoint does not require a large number of supplies. With needle, canvas, and yarn you can begin at any point, and the amount of time and money spent on any one project is a matter of individual choice. Unlike the majority of crafts methods, needlepoint has that happy facility of allowing you to pick it up or put it down at will. Since it is intimately involved with the principle of being decorative and not wholly structural, there is wide leeway for personal expression which is receptive to almost any form the human mind is capable of conceiving.

Today we are not concerned so much with the question of what needlepoint is as with the discovery of new forms and functions for contemporary needlepoint which are distinctly of our time rather than a repetition of that which has already transpired. Ironically, history often provides that fertile source for inspiration which leads to new dimensions.

BRIEF HISTORY

Rich in history and legend, technique and reality, the art of the needle was born of necessity and nurtured by creativity, and served both the material and spiritual aspirations of man. In the annals of time needlework has played a far greater role than merely that of exciting the eye and enticing the senses. From cultures both civilized and uncivilized it has crossed boundaries of both time and culture to preserve a priceless heritage and present a formidable challenge to twentieth-century man. Silent tombs from Asia, Africa, and the Americas, obscured by the ages and reluctant to relinquish their hidden treasures, have yielded forth the endless threads of history to disclose legend, custom and technology.

Examples of fabric displaying the consummate skill with which the ancient Egyptians used needlepoint-like stitches to decorate their woven cloth predate the birth of Christ by more than a thousand years. Within this powerful empire Pharaohs and nobles alike were accustomed to wearing exquisitely embroidered garments and commissioned the execution of large hangings by which to bring added color and beauty into the massive interiors of their palaces.

Biblical references give us a fascinating account of how Egyptian artisans fashioned fine linen sails ablaze with vivid embroideries for their eastern neighbors, the Phoenicians. In these colorful ships, Phoenician traders established the great mart of the Mediterranean. Treasured cargoes of silks, spices, precious stones, coral, gold, purple dye, and richly embroidered fabrics from Sidon were dispensed the length and breadth of the then-known world. We are told of the countless quantities of fine twisted threads dyed violet, purple, and scarlet interlaced with threads of pure gold to produce these embroideries. Acclamation of these gorgeous fabrics was so great that their fame has been recorded for posterity in passages from the Old Testament and the epic works of Homer and Hesiod.

Throughout the ancient world both men and women cultivated a high degree of skill in ornamental needlework, and the heavily jeweled embroideries of Assyria and Babylon can hardly be regarded as less impressive than those of their contemporaries. The fabrics themselves have long since perished, but the ruins from the great palaces at Susa, Nimrud, and Nineveh depict royal figures splendidly attired in garments encrusted by a lavish network of embroidery. Glazed tiles and bas-reliefs portray a veritable kaleidoscope of needlework decorating leather garments, tents, articles of war, umbrellas, and a myriad of other objects used in this culture. Undoubtedly the outstanding character of these ancient embroideries was in large part responsible for stimulating the future development of the beautiful Persian embroideries.

By the time history witnessed the rise of the mighty Greek Empire, long established trade bonds between the Greeks and Phoenicians had given all of Greece access to the luxuries and works of art offered by Asia and the Near East. Soon the works of Greek artisans rivaled those that were imported.

The Greeks' admiration for and cultivation of beauty was in perfect harmony with the high esteem they held for all forms of handiwork. Embroidery was no exception. Needlework was considered to be a gift from the gods. Athena, virgin goddess of wisdom and war, was also the patron goddess who presided over the useful and ornamental arts. Every four years the city of Athens reenacted a great festival in her honor. Days of revelry and rejoicing centered around the solemn ritual of presenting a sacred mantle to the patron goddess in her shrine high atop the Acropolis. A group of carefully selected maidens were charged with the arduous task of embroidering a mantle surpassing all others in beauty and technique. Decoration over the entire body of this garment had to be carried out in a narrative of threads extolling the glories, virtues, and deeds of the beneficent benefactress.

In ancient Greece embroidery was solely the province of women, and Greek women spent many years of their cloistered lives weaving and embroidering for their lords, the deities, and the state. Homer gives us legendary descriptions of the gold-embroidered garments worn by Greek brides, the embroidered mantles for both men and women, and the tasseled robes of Helen of Troy which glistened brightly with shiny threads and were covered overall with resplendent embroideries. Following customary dictates, every household maintained a store of finely wrought fabrics in readiness to be given as gifts and honorary offerings for friends, festivals, and historic events.

Today we are indeed privileged to be able to view a few precious remnants of Greek embroidery. Dating from the 4th century B.C. is the famous collection of Kerch fabrics now in London and more recently the remarkable examples which have come to light from archeological excavations relevant to the Scythian culture.

Commensurate with the complex history of embroidery in the old world were the extraordinary textile achievements in the new world. Long before the first Europeans set foot in the Americas, Pre-Inca cultures in ancient Peru has perfected the development of their textile arts to an amazing degree. The earliest piece of woven pattern found was made more than 2,000 years before the birth of Christ. Almost without exception the fabrics made by these peoples display surprisingly rich and varied techniques which resulted from the consistently high standards, superb craftsmanship, and inventive genius applied to needle and loom. Because of the refined textures, sensitive color combinations, and outstanding use of design elements even the most knowledgeable scholars rank these fabrics among the finest ever made by man.

Sites located south of Paracus Bay contained the largest quantity of embroidered materials. Needles made of thorn, fishbone, wood, and metal were used to fabricate such intricate techniques as knotted and looped network, needleweaving, needle knitting, and embroidery. Decorative yarns of fine wool and cotton were inserted with needles into woven and needle-made fabrics. One very exceptional method used was that of incorporating embroidery stitches into embroidery stitches instead of a woven foundation. Another unusual technique devised was an extension of embroidery which created dimensional figures literally sculpted in the round by means of the knit stitch to project beyond the fabric ground.

Embroidery often covered the entire surface of textiles in flat needlepoint-like stitches so fine they looked like tapestry. It is generally believed that this type of work utilized predetermined patterns marked on a fabric grid mounted on a loom. Evidence such as this strongly suggests that needlepoint as we understand it today may have had its origins with the Pre-Inca peoples.

Constantinople, city of lust, greed, and grandeur, had long been the crossroads of the ancient world. Her strategic geographical location played a decisive role in the evolution of weaving and embroidery in the Western world. For centuries the silks and embroideries of China had been the envy of the ancients. Countless individuals forfeited their lives attempting to transport these precious commodities westward along the great trade routes, and at the dawn of Christianity fine silks were as valuable as gold. Justinian the Great, wise and benevolent ruler of the Byzantine Empire in the 6th century, was responsible for bringing sericulture to the west, and Syrian

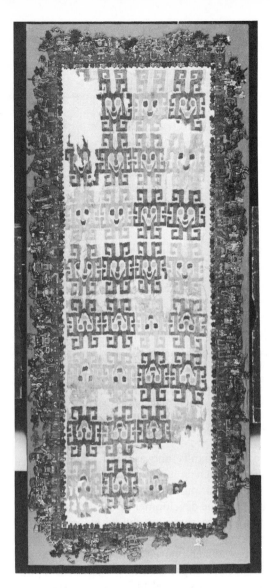

Fig. 1.1 Mantle or ceremonial cloth from Paracus displaying a rectangular body woven in cotton and various colored wool yarns. The entire outer edge of this textile is composed of frieze formed by modeled figures worked in polychrome wool embroidery and loop stitch. Third cent. B.C.

Fig. 1.2 Detail of figures from Fig. 1.2. Courtesy of the Brooklyn Museum.

weavers expanded the scope of weaving by introducing the use of the shuttle.

Imperial workshops in Constantinople manufactured unbelievably rich and elegant fabrics by combining heavily patterned woven grounds with a dazzling array of embroidered details lavishly accented with gold and precious stones. Embroidery worked in a wide range of geometric stitches conformed to highly stylized subject matter. Free use was made of Oriental motifs joined concurrently with pictorial representations of Biblical text to form the predominating modes of design. The total effect was one of such beauty and skill that these fabrics still evoke our interest and admiration.

Strong bonds existed between Byzantium and the East which conditioned a love for the opulent. Rich heavy fabrics received sumptuous decoration that corresponded with the excessive luxury characteristic of the Byzantine court. At the same time such pomp and splendor gave substantial impact to

5

Fig. 1.3. This superb 16th-century chasuble is literally encrusted with Opus Anglicanum and raised embroidery representative of the style which brought enduring fame to the embroideries of the Middle Ages and Renaissance. Museum of Embroideries, Royal Monastery of Guadalupe, Caceras, Spain.

the newly prescribed doctrine of Christianity and established a prototype for royal and ecclesiastical garments which endured for centuries to come.

During the Middle Ages all of Christendom was unified by a religious zeal and dedication to faith which brought the development of needlework to its golden age. Seldom have the fires of creativity burned with such vigor or brillance. Nobleman and commoner, cleric and craftsman were drawn together into a mainstream of activity which poured from the very depths of heart and soul to find its most supreme expression in magnificent Gothic architecture, vibrant stained glass windows, jewel-like enamels, and glowing embroideries dedicated to the glory of God, the remission of sin, and the perpetuation of faith.

Faithful accounts of Biblical stories and the passion of Christ were meticulously embroidered on religious and royal robes or emblazoned in silk threads across the surface of altar frontals, banners, and funeral palls. Stitching approximated perfection because to offer anything less on the altar of God would be unthinkable. Man's art constituted a labor of love which for many was the best and indeed the only wealth they had to give. Nuns, most of whom were descendants of aristocratic families, often devoted entire lifetimes to embroidering vivid documentaries of Biblical history. With needle and threads they stitched priceless records of heroes and heroines, costume and custom interwoven with symbolic interpretation and scriptural dogma.

6 Opus anglicanum or "English work" was the main form of embroidery

practiced from the 11th through the 15th century. Marked by a refined delicacy, this work featured the use of the split stitch. Threads were molded into rhythmic patterns that defined draperies and emphasized anatomical details such as bone and muscle structure, facial contours, and hair styles. Embroidery was frequently used over the whole background. Shimmering grounds solid with gold and silver threads laid on by couching reflected the Byzantine heritage which was so strongly fused into the Gothic style of art. Standards of Oriental splendor had introduced the practice of incorporating gemstones and precious metals into these costly embroideries, which proved to be a significant factor in the destruction of many fine pieces during the ravages of the Counter-Reformation.

Customarily most medieval embroideries were designed by trained craftsman referred to as "needle painters." The mysteries of their craft were jealously guarded within the walls of professional workshops employing both male and female embroiderers. These assistants were required to serve a seven-year apprenticeship before achieving status as artisan. Professional guilds also came into being to protect the artisans and maintain a consistently high level of craftsmanship. In France there were registered embroiderers as early as the year 1295.

Gorgeous embroideries emanated from every corner of Europe, but none could surpass those of England. The demand for English handiwork even extended to the papal court in Rome. Opus Teutonicum or "German work" also became popular at this time. Later to be known as white work, this kind of embroidery had its origin in the heartland of medieval Europe's flax-producing center along the fertile banks of the Rhine and Danube Rivers. Here a durable and evenly woven linen was produced in quantities sufficient to service the needs of the rest of Europe. German work traditionally consisted of linen or white silk threads embroidered on a linen ground with geometric stitches done by counting threads. Saxony gained lasting fame for her beautiful altar frontals, and appreciation for the elegant subtleties of this work insured its survival into the twentieth century.

Praise has always been lavish for the superb craftsmanship and remarkable technique of medieval embroideries, but all too often there are misconceptions about its intention. The austere and somewhat archaic portrayal of human and animal figures are hallmarks of the Gothic style. In true Eastern fashion decoration was based on an ideal and the concept of art for art's sake was nonexistent. Formality and unrealistic imagery confirmed the unearthly nature of these symbolic figures and deliberately set them apart from mortal men. Graphic portrayal on the part of these artisans was in fact so skillful that thousands who could neither read nor write were educated to an ideal, a belief, or an historical fact.

By the 16th century the whole tenor of Western civilization had changed. Europe now possessed a bountiful artistic legacy acquired from the productive genius of the Middle Ages and Renaissance. Material wealth had increased multifold and exposure to Eastern luxuries, coming first by way of the crusaders and then later flowing freely through the rich northern seaports of Venice and Genoa, set a new standard. Great trading centers were established for the exchange of goods in Italy, France, Germany, England

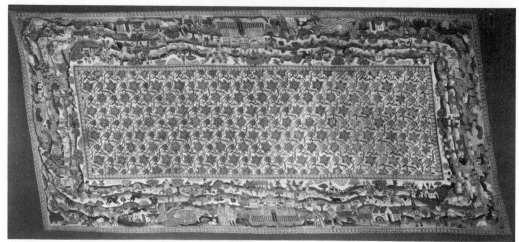

Fig. 1.4 The Bradford Table Carpet is one of the finest examples of English needlework of the 16th century. Worked in tent stitch with colored silks, it is entirely surrounded with a border depicting an historical panorama of country life in this period. Courtesy of the Victoria and Albert Museum, London.

Fig. 1.5 The Great Chamber at Parham Park is dominated by a magnificent four-poster bed adorned with needlework hangings traditionally described as having been worked by Mary Queen of Scots. Courtesy of Parham Park, Sussex, England.

and the low countries. During the long years of occupation in Sicily and Spain, Islamic invaders had given expertise and impetus to a thriving textile industry, and there was a strong preference for Arabic motifs in the decorative arts.

The selfless and complete dedication of individual labor and material wealth to the service and glory of God that prevailed with such fervor during the Middle Ages now became subject to a whole new concept—that of humanism as conceived by Renaissance man. People sought increased gratification of their own desires through personal adornment and environmental comforts. Real splendor and luxury in dress required constant attention to all forms of decorative detail, and individual dwellings often claimed fortunes in the quantity of ornamental textiles required to effect their rich interiors. There was liberal use of tapestry and needlework for walls, cushions, bed hangings, coverlets, and upholstered furniture. Beautiful carpets patterned after those of the Near East were now placed on floors, cupboards, tables, and benches. Only the most splended textiles would suffice, and those which were not imported or commissioned by artisans were worked by the women and servants of the household.

Undoubtedly newly acquired tastes and the abundance of beautiful tapestries had a profound effect on the direction of needlework. Tent stitch came into its own as a separate entity. By covering whole surfaces with this stitch, the necessary durability for cushions and upholstered pieces could be provided. Because of the widespread use of tent stitch for this purpose, it became known as cushion work. Extravagant pieces of needlework emulated the extraordinary details and pictorial imagery characteristic of fine tapestries, but needlework provided a more rapid method of working and could be done on an individual scale.

Needles also made history during this period. The first steel needles were brought to Spain by the Moors in the 14th century. Soon Spain developed a prosperous export business for the quality needles which they manufactured by a process held in greatest secrecy to insure limited competition. Lord Cromwell of England managed to capture the secret, and by 1600 an English guild had been set up for the express purpose of needlemaking. Needles were a treasured commodity which required special housing. Small containers of carved ivory, inlaid woods, precious metals and stones were designed which reached the zenith of imagination and paid tribute to the jeweler's art. Ladies wore their lovely needlecases like jewels suspended from the girdles of their dresses.

Traditionally needlework had been cultivated by great ladies from earliest times, and history gives us an impressive list of 16th and 17th century noblewomen who plied their needles with commendable dexterity. Royal inventories list a staggering number of decorative needleworks imported from Italy and France by Henry VIII, even though his melancholy Spanish queen Catherine of Aragon was a diligent needleworker and is credited with having popularized the style known as black work. Elizabeth I, dauntless stateswoman and superb equestrian, not only left notable examples of canvas work for posterity but also instigated policies which were beneficial to the status of the 16th-century guilds.

Few royal persons are more closely associated with needle and threads than Elizabeth's first cousin, Mary Queen of Scots. Held captive by Elizabeth for most of her adult life, Mary spent much time in the company of the clever needlewoman Elizabeth of Shrewsbury. The stunning array of needlework articles produced by these two women presents a very comprehensive picture of the impressive work of the time.

Customarily great households retained professional designers who organized needlework projects and aided with the finishing details, but the actual needlework was done by the mistress of the house, her retinue of ladies, and her servants. One of the most distinct practices of the period was that of working silk petit point patterns in small motifs or panels on loosely-woven linen canvas which was later applied to a larger cloth of different ground such as satin, velvet, or damask. Quantities of these small pieces were worked and laid in storage until needed. Because of the time lapse and the eclectic quality of these pieces, larger fabrics assembled at a later time were often characterized by a charming selection of random needlework motifs exhibiting unrealistic variance of scale and proportion in the subject matter.

Fig. 1.6 16th and 17th-century needlework purses worked on canvas with silk. Beautiful finishing details are added by way of silk tassels and plaited cords and drawstrings. Courtesy of the Victoria and Albert Museum, London.

Fig. 1.7 The mid-17th-century needlework panel depicting Esther and King Ahasuerus is an excellent example of stump work. Courtesy of the Victoria and Albert Museum, London.

Flowers, fruit, animals, and monograms were favored themes and it was very common to find them intermingled with handsome geometric motifs adapted from carpets and fabrics of the Near East. If several people worked on a large piece of needlework it was usual to find several sets of initials incorporated into the piece.

Turkey work came into vogue because of the compulsion for owning a large number of carpets. Bare floors in estates and manor houses were covered over with leaves, straw, moss, and the like as insulation and to absorb moisture. Carpets were than laid on top. This quaint custom necessitated seasonal moves to facilitate massive housecleaning operations. Historians have left us an interesting and somewhat humorous account of the famous Cardinal Woolsey, who was forced to cover his nose while crossing the courtyard of his own house in order to eliminate the foul odor of rotting compost which covered the floors.

Sixteenth-and seventeenth-century needlework maintained an excellent quality. Many pieces placed emphasis on a narrative theme and became known for the complex details and elaborate gradations of shading. Stitches were very small and consistent, appearing so similar to tapestry technique that needlepoint was called "needle tapestry" for many years to come.

Few sources are more lucrative for viewing the beautiful fabrics and needlework of the Renaissance and Baroque periods than the great paint-

Fig. 1.8 A fascinating array of raised stitches embroidered on a padded satin backing form this exquisite 17th-century mirror frame. Courtesy of the Henry E. Huntington Library and Art Gallery, San Marino, California.

ings. Rembrandt, Rubens, Holbein, Van Eyke, and Titian are but a few of the masters who recorded with meticulous accuracy the personalities and settings typifying this era.

Needlework continued to enjoy unprecedented popularity throughout the 17th and 18th centuries. When the Portuguese opened India to the West in the 16th century, they heralded the beginning of a long line of fortune-seeking merchants who realized enormous fortunes from their profitable cargoes of fragrant spices and herbs, rare woods, porcelain, and finely wrought fabrics of all kinds. Of particular note were the beautiful Indian embroideries and handpainted cottons. Overwhelming enthusiasm for possession of these fabrics the length and breadth of Europe threatened ruination of the domestic market, and as a consequence ownership of these textiles was banned by law.

Indian cottons characteristically displayed the opulent blossoms and graceful lines symbolizing the tree of life. The fresh colors and exotic motifs derived from this image found such favor among the Europeans that it became the prototype for a new style of embroidery known as crewel embroidery. Elements of this design were also borrowed and adapted to needlepoint.

Stump work was by far the most unusual form of needlepoint associated with the 17th and 18th centuries. This so-called new technique was really based on the old idea of working figures on linen or canvas ground and then applying them to another ground with the added attraction of projecting dimensions. Elaborate figures were stuffed, padded or laid over boxwood forms before being attached to the canvas backing. Further ornamentation included satin draperies, bits of lace, human hair, jewels, and satin faces replete with features that had been painstakingly painted or worked with

12

Fig. 1.9 Petit point is used in combination with a variety of other needlepoint stitches to compose an 18th-century allegorical needlework picture. The composition is filled with symbolism and displays a strong influence from the "mille-fleurs" style of tapestry in the background design. Gift of Mrs. Anna Bing Arnold. Courtesy of the Los Angeles county Museum of Art. Photo: Frederick Mollner.

Fig. 1.10 An English Chippendale settee circa 1850 with a walnut frame and needlepoint upholstery. Typical European themes of the periods have been combined with motifs adapted from the imported textiles of India to form the design elements in the needlepoint canvas. Courtesy of the Henry E. Huntington Library and Art Gallery.

13

minute satin stitches. Royal portraits, allegorical and Biblical scenes were favored topics and most were done in the form of pictures which were conceived strictly for decoration.

Stump work was such a novelty that it was not confined for long to just one form and soon it appeared on numerous bits of minutia. The most classic examples are the many ornamental boxes used to house jewels and other treasures. For the first time Europe had become enthralled with surface decoration rather than surface coverings and an element of decadence was introduced into needlework.

Technical perfection became the all-consuming passion of 18th-century needlework. Designers and professional needleworkers were so common that it became an accepted practice for them to supply ready-made designs to shops, which then sold the designs with the corresponding working materials. This was the beginning of needlework kits as we know them today.

Sweeping technological changes resulting from the Industrial Revolution also brought far-reaching modifications in the social, moral, and economic climate of the 19th century. Newly acquired wealth fostered an expanded image of "the lady" who confirmed her prestige and social position through cultivated leisure. The new status of the middle and upper middle class male dictated that monetary and domestic contributions in the form of housework were degrading. Woman's place was in the home, but she no longer held an essential position in the national economy. Instead she was required to fulfill standards based on the idea of woman as ornament to her husband. Domestic work and child care were relegated to paid employees in order to free milady for the more important issues of the day such as painting, music, reading, and various kinds of plain and fancy needlework.

Decorative needlework became subject to mass consumption. It was an ever-present occupation with all ladies at both public and private gatherings. To facilitate this vogue a need arose for small carrying cases in which to

Fig. 1.11 The charm, vitality, and freshness captured by Phoebe Kriebel in her needlepoint picture titled "Township" remain timeless. Wool on canvas, circa 1857.

house and transport one's work. Quantities of beautifully conceived cases were designed to answer this need. The wide variety, fine quality, and unusual design of these bags adds a distinctive note to the period which in itself warrants further study.

Berlin work ushered in a whole new era of needlepoint. All of Europe and American was caught up in the craze for this new style, which was destined to enjoy great popularity for more than half a century. In fact, remnants of Berlin work remain to this very day in the form of painted canvases and kits which are featured in leading department stores and yarn shops.

In its most literal sense Berlin work was canvas embroidery worked in Berlin wools by means of copying a color chart known as a Berlin pattern. In general the term Berlin work covered a much broader range of needlework including the application of any kind of thread or beads to a Berlin pattern and the various other handicrafts using Berlin wools.

The most dedicated advocates of Berlin work were the fashionable middle- and upper-class Victorian ladies in England, but everyone from the Queen on down became addicted to it. History had presented the ideal set of circumstances to insure its success.

Berlin work brought a new color and excitement that fulfilled a very real physical and psychological need for ladies of this time. It was an activity that met prevailing criteria for a woman who aspired to gentility and refinement. Countless hours could be spent making needlework objects which had both utilitarian and artistic value for self, family, and home. The basic technique employed in Berlin work was so simple and direct that everyone was encouraged to participate. Most important of all the "newness" of color and design approach had an irresistible appeal.

German wools had a soft, fleecy quality which made them extremely receptive to dyes, and the color range was dazzling. Reputedly Berlin wools were manufactured in more than a thousand colors. Never before had such brilliance been seen.

The accessibility of ready-made patterns and painted canvases offered the unartistic lady artistic designs en masse. Prior to this time needlework patterns existed in a limited number of scarce and expensive printed books or as custom work. The only alternative was to secure traditional patterns passed on from family or friends. Painted canvases opened up new avenues of imagery. Great paintings, floral scenes, and romantic interpretations of recently discovered archeological finds were exactingly copied on canvas and offered escape from the dull, drab surroundings of interiors and overcrowded cities. Until 1842 any design could be copied without permission and wholesale pirating became the order of the day.

In 1856 William Henry Perkin invented the first aniline dyes, and the novelty of magenta and mauve became a fashion rage. Artifical dyes had opened the way for an ever-expanding color palette, but unfortunately much that remains from this period does not give us an accurate picture of the original colors. Many dye colors were beautiful, but others were garish to say the least. Environment, soil, and weather caused changes in the original substance of these unstable dyes and remaining color schemes often appear tasteless and offensive to modern eyes. Too, the concept of bril-

Fig. 1.12 Peasant costumes all over the world have remained relatively unchanged for hundreds of years. Geometric stitching or counted work in brightly colored threads, such as the needlework seen above, is commonly used to form decoration. In this early 20th-century costume from Afghanistan, beadwork, tent stitch, and cross stitch, first introduced from the Greek Islands in early times, have been combined in a very individual manner with coins, small pearl buttons, and a modern-day zipper head. Gift of Mrs. George Brandow. Courtesy of the Los Angeles County Museum of Art. Photo: Frederick Mollner.

Fig. 1.13 Detail of needlework shown in Fig. 1.14. Photo: Frederick Mollner.

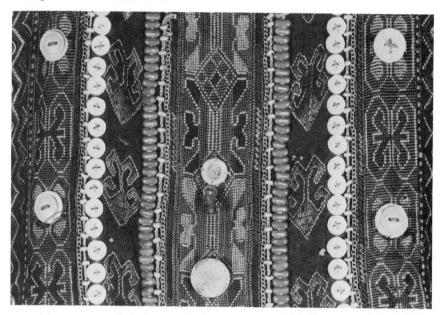

liance was a new phenomenon and difficult to handle. Before aniline dyes were introduced, all colors were derived from animal, vegetable, or mineral sources; the resulting hues were seldom harsh and blended easily. Beaded work is less subject to the ravages of time, and it is from the profusion of beaded trifles made during this time that we are able to discern with more accuracy the prevailing color schemes.

The earliest known Berlin work was done in silks on very fine canvas which encouraged the working of delicate designs. Many of these early pieces are quite lovely. With the increasing pressure of mass appeal, Berlin work was adapted to all kinds of articles in many different materials. Beads, wook, silk, chenille, and even twisted paper were employed to decorate everything in sight. Artificial flowers, enshrined mementos, pictures, fire screens, and various pieces of upholstered furniture blossomed forth in glowing needlepoint to occupy every nook and cranny of the Victorian household. Personal regalia sported needlepoint achievements in the form of face screens, purses, decorated bodices, fans, garters, cigar cases, and much, much more.

As the fetish for Berlin work progressed, individuals relied less and less on their own choices in color and design and preferred instead to pursue that which was stylish. Eventually years of increasing rigidity, conscious imitation, and endless repetition hastened the impending decline of needlework. This once valid and creative art form had become little more than an inferior craft.

At the beginning of the 20th century a reexamination had already started taking place to reestablish needlework as art. Marked concern was felt for the cultural and economic loss brought about by the decline of needlework in the Western world. Government-sponsored schools were set up in England and on the continent to upgrade standards, perpetuate tradition, and encourage new forms of needlework expression. Societies came into being for the express purpose of preserving and motivating all phases of needlework handicrafts. The gifted and the curious found a new awareness and appreciation for an old art in new context. Time alone will determine the ultimate boundaries to be realized by this inquiring spirit.

2 Designing Your Own

Needlepoint is work. Developing a game of golf or cooking a gourmet meal is also work. Effort and application are required on your part to do any of these things, but each one has its own very special kind of enjoyment and reward. In contrast to many other activities, the time and effort devoted to working a piece of needlepoint results in an article that can, and often does, outlive its creator. In light of the time invested and the enduring nature of your work, it is both logical and appropriate to consider seriously designing your own canvases. Planning and participating in a project from beginning to end not only guarantees a "one of a kind," but it will also cut your monetary investment almost in half. Another advantage of designing your own needlepoint is that you have absolute control over the size, color, subject matter, and raw materials that go into its make-up. When you start designing your own work, you have begun the transition from a working hobby to a productive art form.

Fig. 2.1 (Opposite, top) Working graph for Victorian House.

Fig. 2.2 (Opposite, bottom) Needlework panel of Victorian House in Fig. 2.1. Designed and worked by Ginny Ross. Photograph by Brian Gaines.

DESIGN: DEFINITION

What Is Design? In the most literal sense, design is the selection and arrangement of visual elements for order with interest. Defined in broader terms, design is human expression formulated by our individual responses to all that we know, see, and experience.

This concept of design is applicable in general to any form of art or craft including needlepoint design. A more specific definition evolves when design is considered relative to one particular art or craft.

Traditionally, needlepoint has been a decorative art in which craftsmanship, content, and materials are joined in harmonious union to create an object or article destined for eventual use. Considered from this standpoint, the final design form established for any needlepoint canvas is determined to a large extent by the ultimate purpose the piece is to serve. The decorative content should always be an integral part of the object, enhancing and emphasizing both its form and purpose.

Where Is Design? When most people ask the question, "Where is design?" they are really asking, "Where can I find the source of design?" Design exists within the individual. Designing is the art of transforming individual ideas and experiences into tangible form. Sources for design are everywhere.

The artist has learned to discover ideas from every facet of life. Imagination and curiosity motivate interpretation of what has been seen and felt in

Fig. 2.3. Painting "Three Workmen" by Gray Phillips.

Fig. 2.4 The intriguing shapes and mood set by California artist Gray Phillips in his painting "Three Workmen" inspired this imaginative needlework picture by Helen Kline Phillips of Lookout Mountain, Tennessee.

the form of design. Many people possess an instinctive feeling for design; an empty canvas or the desire for a beautiful and unique chair seat or pillow signals a challenge to design. Others may feel that they have "no talent," or that their background and experience are too limited to attempt a design on canvas. Such feelings should not be allowed to deter potential ability. Anyone who really wants to develop a design for canvaswork can do so. If you have a little patience and a sincere desire to learn, the first step has already been taken toward making your own original needlepoint designs.

No steadfast rules exist for creating a good design, but an excellent way to begin is by knowing the basic elements embodied in all valid forms of design. These elements can be thought of as the artistic tools by which to build a design. Learning to recognize and use them will not only aid in producing a more effective design, but at the same time a whole new world of design will be opened to you.

THE ELEMENTS OF DESIGN

SHAPE

Shape is the most easily recognizable element in design. An infinite number and variety of shapes fill space in our universe, from the shape of the book you are reading to the shapes formed by the planets and constellations themselves. Four sources provided the basis for our concept of shape.

Natural shapes are those shapes occuring in nature. While impossible to duplicate, their subtle complexities of form and endless cycles of change have provided a fertile design source for every age.

Geometric shapes are man-made shapes composed of straight lines, angles, and curves. Geometric shapes are characteristically expressive of objects in a man-made environment, such as buildings, pyramids, machines, and furniture. The very angular shapes comprising the ground of your

Fig. 2.5 Coiled shell. Photo: Frederick Mollner.

Fig. 2.6 Apache coil basket. Photo: Frederick Mollner.

Fig. 2.7 House of Shells, Salamanca, Spain. Photo: Jeanne Schnitzler.

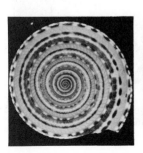

Fig. 2.8. Photogram. Frederick Mollner.

Fig. 2.9 Pen and ink drawing of "Geometric Shapes." Jeanne Schnitzler.

Fig. 2.10 Pen and ink drawing of Abstract Shapes." Jeanne Schnitzler.

canvas immediately indicate that geometric shapes offer a safe and appropriate basis on which to design a canvas.

Abstract shapes are derived from a recognizable object or thing that has been distorted or simplified to enhance the design quality. All forms of art contain some degree of abstraction.

Nonobjective shapes are shapes in which no object can be recognized. They can and often are an interpretation of a feeling or emotion. Many nonobjective shapes are found in nature, such as patterns resulting from weathering or erosion, water movement, and the markings on flowers, fruits, and vegetables.

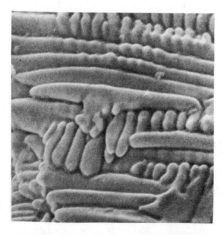

Fig. 2.11 Many non-objective shapes can be seen in this magnification of a weld. Photo: Frederick Mollner.

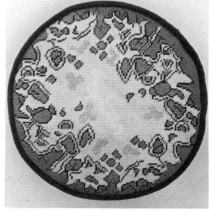

Fig. 2.12 Non-objective shapes form the theme for this needlework pillow.

Line is movement recorded by graphic means. All forms of human expression relate to line. Line is found in many forms; it delineates and encloses shape, records and establishes movement, and is used to create pattern within a unit or to make up the unit itself.

Fig. 2.13   The beautiful and sensitive
use of line is evident in Arabic Kufic
and Japanese calligraphy.

Fig. 2.14   Line defines a network of pattern and shape in a
dragonfly wing.

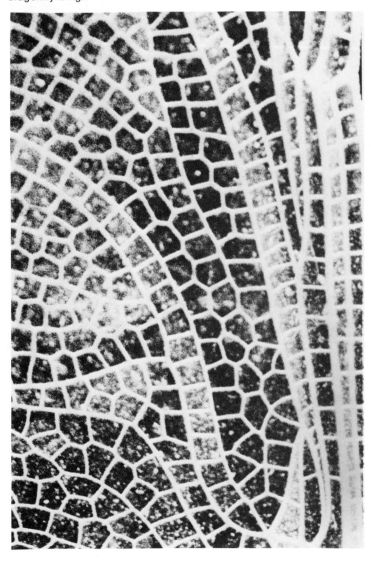

Fig. 2.15 Spiderweb. Photo: Mert Cramer.

Fig. 2.16 Line patterns in a building. Photo: Frederick Mollner.

Fig. 2.17 The lines formed by the lights of oncoming cars on a rainy night express tension, chaos, and aggravation. Photo: Frederick Mollner.

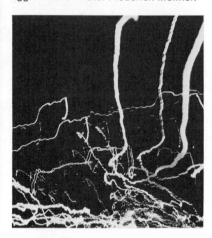

Fig. 2.18 "Study of a Tree" by Claude Lorrain. Norton Simon Inc. Foundation, Los Angeles. In skillful hands lines can be made to interpret a mood or capture the essence of all things.

Fig. 2.19 American craftsman Polly Goodman composed an entire work titled "Op II" with line. In her composition lines interrelate and collect to make shape, create movement, develop texture, and project the illusion of advancing and receding planes. Courtesy of the American Crafts Council.

In addition to the many forms line takes, it also has many different qualities. There are thick, bold lines and thin, delicate lines. Angular lines are rigid and often chaotic, while curved lines are graceful and flowing. The lines in design become an important factor in how we view or read a design. Line creates shape and makes pattern.

24

Horizontal lines are strong and stabilizing.

Vertical lines are active and tend to move in an upward direction.

Jagged and diagonal lines are turbulent and hard to control.

Curved lines are soft and easy and often act as a unifying force.

TEXTURE

Texture is the variation in a surface that stimulates our sense of touch. Rough bark on a tree; the smooth, cool exterior of stainless steel; the soft, fuzzy nap of yarn: all are textures that can be both seen and felt. There is another type of texture called *implied texture*. Implied texture is surface modulation that is seen but not felt. Needlepoint presents an ideal medium in which the designer can use texture to create exciting surface enrichment and great versatility in canvaswork.

Fig. 2.20 Photo: Frederick Mollner.

Fig. 2.21 Photo: Ben Makuta.

Fig. 2.22 Weathering results in an unusual variety of textural effects. Photo: Don Urquidi.

Fig. 2.23 Designer Peter Ashe displays an admirable use of proportion and space by scaling the details and shapes of a Victorian house to fit the oblong dimension of a bell pull.

Size establishes the relationship of the various parts to one another within a given design. It sets up automatic comparisons between neighboring units, between all of the design elements as a whole, and between design elements as they correlate to the overall dimensions of composition. When using this principle of relationships between sizes you are establishing proportion in your work.

Size is one of the most important elements in good design and it is also the one element with which the beginning needlepoint designer has greatest difficulty. Seldom is a design too large for the space contained on the canvas ground. Usually just the opposite is true; there is too much space and not enough design. Think of your canvas as a conquest of space, then plan for visual proportion.

One quick way to estimate visual proportion is by cutting or tearing pieces of paper that approximate the size and mass of your final work, then placing the paper shapes into a tentative arrangement on your canvas ground. At this stage of designing, adjustments and changes for the final design are relatively easy to make. Just these few moments spent in the planning stage could mean saving you from endless hours of work or from the completion of an end product that is disappointing at best.

COLOR

Color is the most flexible of all the elements in design. It plays a broad and significant role in every needlepoint design by determining the character of the design and conditioning psychological response (see color plates 2 through 6). Nature gives us an unending panorama of color from which we can learn a great deal. Close observation of natural objects will reveal the amazing variation and exquisite quality to be found in the world of color. Man, too, has and is developing an ever expanding pallet of color. Our increased awareness of and concern with color has created a desire for further knowledge and direction to aid us in the personal selection and control of color. Due to the importance and complex nature of this one element is design, Chapter 5 has been devoted elusively to the study of color as it applies to needlepoint design.

USING THE ELEMENTS OF DESIGN

Once you are familiar with the elements or tools of design, start designing. It is not necessary to use all of the elements each time that you develop a design, but it is important to understand the possibilities each one can offer in forming a more effective design. Suggestions for some of the many ways in which it is possible to use the design elements are contained in the following section on principles of design. These principles do not constitute a formula for good design, but they do act as directives to help you organize

Fig. 2.24 Sister Mary Helena makes beautiful use of pattern and rhythmic stitches to lead the viewer's eye upward to the expressive faces of her figures in the work titled "The Visitation." Courtesy of the American Crafts Council.

a more satisfying and innovative end product. Awareness of the interaction among the principles and elements of design will answer in part your questions about what design is and where to find it. At the same time, you will be acquiring a firm foundation upon which to develop your own individual approach to needlepoint design.

THE PRINCIPLES OF DESIGN

The *eventual use and placement* of your needlepoint will be a major criterion in establishing what kind of design and how much design will be chosen to fill the space on your canvas. Select design elements for *unity*. Unity in design results when the individual elements which make up the design relate or belong to one another. Give them something in common, such as size, shape, texture, or color.

Add clarity, meaning, and interest to your design by making one element dominate. *Dominance* results when one color, one line, one shape, or one idea is given more prominence in the design than any other. In the overall pattern, dominance of or focus on a single element within each motif or unit creates emphasis and importance. Pictorial compositions need dominance to create and maintain a center of interest and establish the theme.

Entice the eye with *rhythm*. Rhythm is an indispensible component to the vitality and flow of a good design. When rhythm is introduced into a work a definite plan for movement results. Rhythm is associated with and activated by variety.

Variety is the magical ingredient that draws people to the corners of the earth in search of something new and different. It is also the key factor in adding distinctive character and individuality to your work. Variety is easily achieved in needlepoint through the wide selection of color, shapes,

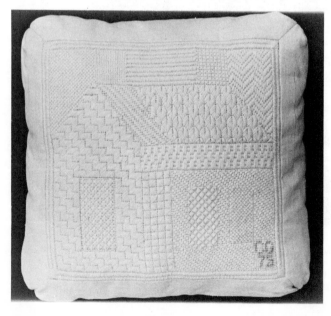

Fig. 2.25 Rhythm and pattern dominate as elements when white wool stitches are skillfully placed on a white ground to develop a pictorial image and project a decorative impact which is both elegant and refined in mood. Designed by Marian Natham. Stitched by Carol Goddard.

Fig. 2.26 Inge Woolley's adaptation of an Imari design illustrates symmetrical balance.

Fig. 2.27 Theresa Lee of Lee's Art Studio, Cherry Hill, N.J., uses asymmetric balance in a needlework picture developed in the style of a Japanese print.

textures, and techniques available to the designer. Think of variety in terms of contrast: light to dark, bright to dull, large to small, complex to simple, or textured to plain. Look beneath the obvious and choose your subject matter with a selective eye; the common will become uncommon, but only when it is handled with care. Too much variety produces confusion, and too little variety results in monotony.

Decisions regarding how much or how little variety is needed within a specific design are most often the result of an instinctive reaction prompted by our basic need for *aesthetic balance*. Aesthetic balance comes into play when the power and sparkle of a warm, vibrant color are counterbalanced with a large area of cool, subtle color; or when a large group of small shapes lend support to one large shape; or again when fast movement in one direction is stabilized by movement in a contrasting direction. Nature has taught us that balance is an indispensable law to the natural order of all things. Since design is first and foremost a plan for order, it demands balance.

In a broader context, balance results from the arrangement of elements to neutralize opposing forces and distribute the weight of the design elements within a total work. Consideration of balance in its larger sense implies two kinds of compositional balance; symmetrical balance and asymmetrical balance. Symmetrical balance occurs when a work is divided into two equal parts with each part containing an identical number and size of objects. Symmetrical balance is often referred to as formal balance. Asymmetrical balance occurs when the two halves of a work are unequal in size and weight. This type of balance is usually more interesting because it is less rigid and obvious. Japanese prints have long been famed for their outstand-

29 ing use of asymmetric balance.

Fig. 2.28 A striking pillow employs the theory of decorative yarn work associated with the Aran Isles. Designed by Ginny Ross.

SOME BASIC APPROACHES TO CREATIVE DESIGN

DESIGN BY STRUCTURE

One of the most appealing attributes of needlepoint is its immediacy. It is this one characteristic above all others that challenges anyone who picks up a needle, a length of yarn, and a scrap of canvas to create a personalized, original, and unique needlepoint design. You do not need to have drawing skill or in-depth background to design by structure; you do need to have a large measure of curiosity and a genuine desire to explore the many combinations to which your needle and yarn might lead. Experimentation with just a few stitches will indicate at once the almost limitless number of design forms possible in needlework. By grouping and organizing the stitches worked into the canvas, exciting units and motifs can be formed, or structured, which are the direct result of technique and do not depend on preconceived sketches or paintings which must be adapted to the canvas.

One kind of stitch grouped in sequence immediately begins to from a rhythmic pattern or well-defined shape. Design evolves when this shape or pattern is given variation in size or arrangement. Additional complexity and interest can be introduced by variation in color and texture. Many beautiful and fascinating pieces of needlework have resulted from this very simple structural approach.

When you are planning to design a piece of needlework through structuring, start by getting to know your materials. Look closely at the ground. Woven ground forms the foundation upon which all needlework is applied. The canvas or fabric upon which you choose to work is made up of a continuous series of squares of predetermined size. All needlework is predicated on this absolute module; the square is paramount. Acknowledgment of the need for an intimate understanding of the nature of the square will expedite a more innovative and satisfactory end product.

Some view the rigid sides and static dimensions of the square as a stifling restriction. Others find the perfect balance and angular proportions of this shape a stimulating challenge to see new dimensions and interesting divisions. Herein lies the secret to creative needlepoint. As surely as any square contains four equal sides, it also contains the potential for being divided into triangles, or joined with a mate to compound rectangles of varying lengths and definite directions.

To start, select yarn compatible in thickness and weight with your canvas and begin by working out a few simple motifs. Start small: use a small piece of the same fabric or canvas you anticipate using in your final work and select one color of yarn. Complexities can always be introduced later. This type of experimentation carried out on a small scale will serve the same function a notebook or sketch pad does in other types of artistic endeavor: it gives you the opportunity to "play" with ideas at the same time you are gaining greater insight into the characteristics of your materials. Design motifs can be developed quickly to form a base upon which to build a finished design, and all the while there is a margin for error that does not risk the ruination of quantities of expensive materials.

In this preliminary study the key work is *experiment.* Let your imagination run riot. Try placing small stitches next to larger stitches, or solid areas of stitches next to broken areas of stitches. Make identical groups of stitches that go in different directions. Compound a shape by using several kinds of stitches. Add a change of pace by introducing another color.

Find out what your yarn can do. Twist it, loop it, or even apply areas of cut pile. Rhythm and pattern can be enhanced by playing plain or flat surfaces against richly textured areas. Raised areas can easily be made by using several strands of yarn at the same time. This kind of surface modulation activates tactile sensations and effects interesting shadow play.

Try allowing the ground to make a visible design contribution. Unfortunately, this is one aspect of canvaswork that has been consigned to all but oblivion. Generations of conditioning have nurtured the fetish that the only correct way of working canvas is by engulfing it in a solid sea of yarn so meticulously applied that even the needle holes are rendered invisible or hidden under a clever disguise. Interestingly enough, there are a number of beautifully executed works from medieval and Renaissance periods featuring decorative needle holes as an integral part of the design. Outstanding textiles from pre-Incan Peru have long been renowned for the exquisite

Fig. 2.29 The contemporary weaving "Lost and Proud" by artist-craftswoman Lenore Tawney gains dynamic design impetus and a highly distinctive character from her unique handling of exposed warp. Courtesy of the American Crafts Council.

Fig. 2.30 Peruvian gauze weave featuring cotton embroidery on an open weave grid. Wrapped and knotted weft. Costume Council Fund, courtesy of the Los Angeles County Museum of Art.

Fig. 2.31 Peruvian gauze weave executed in cotton from Chancay, central Peru (1101-1410 A.D.) John Wise Collection. Costume Council Fund Purchase. Courtesy of the Los Angeles County Museum of Art.

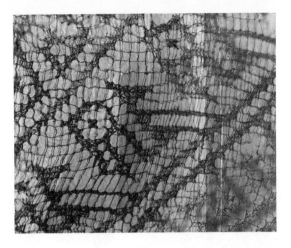

Fig. 2.32   Detail of Fig. 2.45

examples of gauze weaving in which needlework or needle weaving was interlaced on a ground of gauze net.

In all forms of canvaswork, both the ground and the needle holes are a reality. They can and do make a positive contribution as valid design elements to needlework composition. Controlled sections of exposed canvas give dramatic contrast to heavily worked areas. Great delicacy and added emphasis can be achieved when an open grid is allowed to penetrate a given motif. This design approach unites ground and subject area into an integrated whole, and by so doing the two elements activate and support one another. Needle perforations function in a similar manner. When used in quantity throughout a design, they form a strong parallel to the technique commonly known as pulled or drawn work. Needle holes used in combination with a solid repetitive pattern create a staccato outline around each seg-

Fig. 2.33   This elegant 18th-century fan displays a linen ground covered entirely with pulled work and embroidery (France, Germany, or Denmark, 1730s-1740s). Courtesy of the Cooper-Hewitt Museum of Decorative Arts and Design, Smithsonian Institution.

Fig. 2.34   Cut work, hollie, needlepoint lace, geometrical satin, and back-stitches grace this exquisite white linen sampler bearing the inscription "Marthe Arron 1734." Courtesy of the Royal Ontario Museum, Toronto.

ment of the pattern. A tightly structured pattern or motif using needle holes in continuous sequence results in an effect simulating open work.

Both needle holes and exposed canvas produce work that is highly decorative in quality but less durable and practical than that using a solidly worked ground. Technically, such work does not provide the necessary utilitarian requirements for pieces subject to constant or heavy use. Artistically, its decorative value could be a great asset in pieces such as wall hangings, table covers, pillows, and garments.

Fig. 2.35   Snow crystals. Photo: W.A. Bentley.

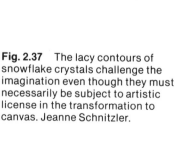

Fig. 2.36   Graphed snowflakes. Jeanne Schnitzler.

Fig. 2.37   The lacy contours of snowflake crystals challenge the imagination even though they must necessarily be subject to artistic license in the transformation to canvas. Jeanne Schnitzler.

Fig. 2.38   Pulled work sampler designed and worked by Ginny Ross.

At this point you should be ready to contemplate a design by structure. Since this approach employs and emphasizes the basic concept that the character of the stitches themselves is the substance of all forms of needlework, it is one of the purest forms of design you can use in developing a needlepoint canvas. Good design in any medium is expressive of the elements from which it is compounded. For these reasons, it follows that there are definite advantages and disadvantages that you should be aware of before you begin a work using this approach.

Advantages
1. Your design is an outgrowth of participation and does not rely on outside sources.
2. Innovation is limited only by imagination and technical limitations.
3. This approach guarantees an end product that is true to the inherent dignity of needlepoint and could not be duplicated in any other medium.

Disadvantages
1. Design is limited to geometric and abstract forms.
2. Structural interest can be weakened by the introduction of too much color.
3. Creativity must be adjusted to terms compatible with the end product.

DESIGNING FROM NATURE

Nature has been an unending source of inspiration to all people in all places since the dawn of time. Thousands and thousands of years ago, we reacted to the work around us, and through the ages every civilization has continued to react to natural phenomena, by reaffirming our roots in nature and seeking to develop in harmony with it.

The rich panorama of color, patterns, textures, and shapes found in natural forms provides abundant means by which to stimulate creative design. Look about you. Inspiration from natural forms is as close as the contents of your refrigerator or the view from your nearest window. There you will find familiar objects that are seen every day but seldom really studied. A closer look can be the beginning of a design.

NATURE FROM A PHOTOGRAPH

The person who feels unable to design or uncomfortable about designing directly from nature can readily achieve success with an easy procedure that will result in a personalized design for canvas.

Take a picture of a natural object, such as a flower, a fruit, an insect, or some leaves. Choose something you enjoy and confront it head on. For a beginning project, select objects that are relatively simple in structure and offer some contrast in color. After your photograph is developed, have it enlarged. From this enlargement, make a direct tracing of the subject matter you wish to use in your design. The design is then ready to be transferred to the canvas (see Chapter 4).

Fig. 2.39 Magnolia. Photo: Ginny Ross

Fig. 2.40 Tracing of Fig. 2.56

Once you have discovered how readily adaptable this method can be for developing your own designs, consider the possibilities for expanding it. Add greater complexity and variety to your designs by combining the subject matter from several photographs into one design.

Fig. 2.41 Thistle. Photo: Frederick Mollner.

Fig. 2.42 Drawing of a thistle. Frederick Mollner.

Fig. 2.43 Photo: Frederick Mollner.

Fig. 2.44 Drawing of three thistles. Frederick Mollner.

Fig. 2.45   Photo: David McNutt.

Fig. 2.46   Drawing of a bumble bee.
Frederick Mollner.

Fig. 2.47   Composite drawing.
Frederick Mollner.

At this point, you are ready to decide upon the quality and quantity of color to be used. Some people enjoy developing the color scheme while the work is in progress, using a flexible approach that allows for a change of mind. Others prefer color guidelines. On a large piece of work some preliminary color plan is desirable, both from the standpoint of estimating the approximate yarn costs involved and as an aid in avoiding the possibility of variance in dye lots that often occurs with yarn purchased over a period of time.

There are several methods for making a color plan, of which two follow:

1. Make a duplicate tracing of the final design and add color with paint, crayon, or colored pens. This plan will show you the exact amount and placement of color and allows for adjustments before investing in experience yarns. It also serves as a reference while you work.
2. Paint the canvas with acrylic paints in the desired color scheme. You will immediately see how the color will look on the finished piece (see Chapter 3 on painting the canvas).

Design Directly from Natural Objects

Be original. Although there are few designs that can be said to be "original" in the sense that at sometime, someone somewhere has not used them before, originality in design does not depend so much on the source as on the way in which each individual sees and interprets that source. Each person extracts those aspects from an object or experience that have personal significance to her or him. It is this individual interpretation that makes design creative, exciting, and original.

Start simply. Begin by selecting one object: a fruit, a vegetable, or a flower. Look at it closely. List your immediate observations on a scrap of paper. Now ask yourself some questions. What kind of shape does it have?

37

Fig. 2.48 From "Studies of a Pomegranate" by Donna Inaba. Photo: Frederick Mollner. Figs. 2.49 through 2.57 are part of the same study.

Fig. 2.49

Does it contain one shape or many shapes? Is it hard or soft, solid or porous, shiny or dull?

Try making some preliminary sketches. Draw your object from different angles and in different kinds of light. Shadow forms not only simplify the shape of an object, but they also form interesting shapes themselves. Change and distort some of the shapes you find. Take your object apart and study the inside segments or parts. See how smaller shapes form and collect to create the large outer shape. As you are observing the shapes, be aware of the many kinds of color and textures contained in just one object. That which at first may appear to be just a simple apple, orange, or daisy is, in reality, a very interesting and complex structure. Analyze and reassemble the many parts you see into a composition.

In your planning, do not neglect to view your object from a different perspective. Take a bird's-eye view or a caterpillar's view. Such exploration can suggest new and unexpected possibilities for design directions.

Fig. 2.50   Fig. 2.51   Fig. 2.52

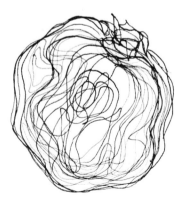

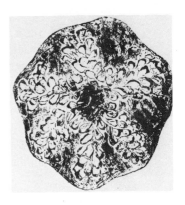

Fig. 2.53

Fig. 2.54

Fig. 2.55

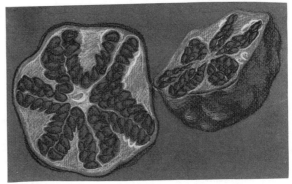

Fig. 2.56

Fig. 2.57

Cut Paper

Another very valuable technique used to develop design is working with cut paper. One of the most interesting aspects of natural form is that almost every object in nature can be interpreted by a geometric shape. Cut paper lends itself to developing simple and direct shapes that can easily be moved around into pleasing arrangements.

Cut large shapes and small shapes. Cut or tear shapes that suggest the various parts of your object. Segment shapes, overlap shapes, and superimpose shapes; arrange and rearrange them until they begin to form an interesting composition. You will soon discover that by combining geometric shapes based on organic forms, a fresh and exciting approach to design will be opened especially for the person who "cannot draw a thing."

KEEPING A REFERENCE FILE

One of the most important things you can do when creating your own designs is to keep a file of ideas. This is very simple and most interesting. **39** Basically, every time you see something exciting, you should clip it out and file it. You may find a picture of an animal with a fascinating expression, a beautiful butterfly, or a superb flower. Although you may never use any of these ideas, they will be a constant source of inspiration and all sorts of ideas can evolve from them.

At first you will be able to keep them in a large envelope, but probably you will soon accumulate too many for this and will have to secure some sort of system. The temporary file boxes that can be purchased in a stationery store are excellent. Some typical file categories might be birds, animals, children, fruits, flowers, contemporary design, traditional design, or any special areas of interest to you, your family, or your situation.

This might seem totally unnecessary to you, but, there is nothing more frustrating to anyone than to want to design a canvas but have absolutely no idea where to begin. If you would like to draw a giraffe but have no picture to look at, then it is virtually impossible to do so. Yet in the course of one year you might have seen scores of pictures of giraffes.

Fig. 2.58 Design on this pillow is called a mirror image. One-half of the design is drawn and then the pattern is reversed. In this manner, both sides of the design will be identical. Designed and executed by Geri Kurek.

Fig. 2.59 Magnified X-ray view of a moth. Photo: Frederick Mollner.

SOURCES FOR DESIGN IDEAS

Take another point of view. Don't be satisfied to know an object, place, or thing from just one perspective. Seek to discover all the unique and exciting aspects of your subject matter with the aid of twentieth-century technology.

Seek exposure to other art forms through books, museums, and travel. The motivation gained from developing a familiarity with other avenues of artistic expression can easily lead to a lifetime adventure; the more you design and observe, the more aware you become of the constant interaction and interrelationships existing among the arts. Art becomes self-perpetuating, and artistic expression provides impetus for more artistic expression. This concept of action and reaction is centuries old and can readily be seen in both contemporary and historical sources.

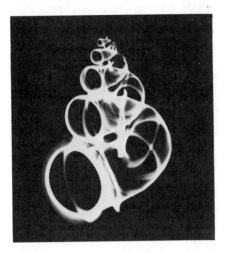

Fig. 2.60 The sum of the parts can be arranged into a fascinating whole when chosen by a selective eye. Consider using an X-ray view, for example (Figs. 2.60 and 2.61). Books on science, medicine, and photography often contain illustrations of this type. Periodicals and journals relating to these field are also likely prospects. Photo courtesy of John Nesson and Michael D. Smith.

Fig. 2.61 Courtesy of John Nesson and Michael D. Smith.

Fig. 2.62 An aerial view presents a new concept of spatial relationships and a multiplicity of forms. Courtesy of California State University at Los Angeles.

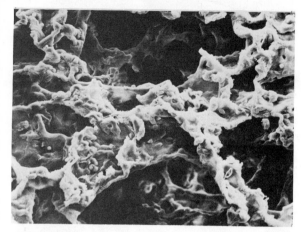

Fig. 2.63 The ordinary becomes the extraordinary when viewed under a microscope and can lead to a whole new dimension in design.
Photographs of lung tissue courtesy of Stuart Ackerman, V.A. Hospital, Palo Alto, California.

Fig. 2.64

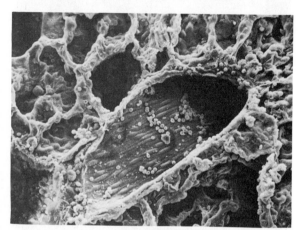

Fig. 2.65

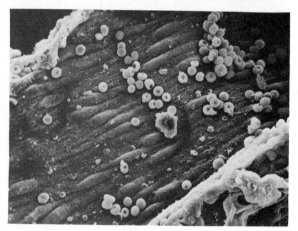

Fig. 2.66 Find another angle. Look under things, over things, and into things. Look for your own "right way" to interpret what you see and feel.

Fig. 2.67 Photo: Don Urquidi.

Fig. 2.68 This beautiful rug, patterned after a traditional oriental prayer rug, uses a mirhab as a central theme that closely resembles the mirhab in Fig. 2.96. Designed and executed by Irene Rosta.

Fig. 2.69 Mirhab in the Court of the Dolls, Alcazar, Seville, Spain. Photo: Jeanne Schnitzler.

Fig. 2.70 The 20th-century painter Piet Mondrian dedicated himself to a search for art in its purest form. "Composition in Red, Blue and Yellow" (1937-42, cil on canvas, 23¾ by 21⁷/₈') captures the essence of his artistic expression. The Sidney and Harriet Janis Collection. Gift to The Museum of Modern Art, New York.

Fig. 2.71 This new approach to purity of form in the visual arts inspired noted designer Yves St. Laurent to creat a collection of garments in 1963 based on the paintings by Piet Mondrian. Copyright © 1965 by The Conde Nast Publications, Inc. Courtesy *Vogue.*

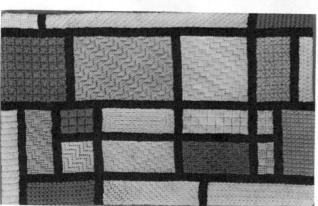

Fig. 2.72 The geometric purity of Mondrian's work has also found a variety of interpretations in needlework. Designed and executed by Ginny Ross. Illuminated manuscripts, tapestries, paintings, stained glass windows, and porcelain and excellent sources for design.

Fig. 2.73 Antique Imari bowl. (Leave extra line for credits). Courtesy Inge Woolley, Creative Needle.

Fig. 2.74 An antique Imari bowl displaying the phoenix symbol of the empress's beauty and peace inspired an exquisitely detailed needlework picture by designer Inge Woolley, Creative Needle.

Fig. 2.75 The art and artifacts from primitive cultures are emblazoned with a rich and seemingly endless profusion of exotic designs, symbols, and patterns. Stone stela with image of Mayan priest. Tikal, Guatemala. Photo: Jeanne Schnitzler.

Fig. 2.76 Wall hanging featuring an adaptation of the figures from the Aztec calendar. Designed by Ginny Ross. Stitched by Margaret Tullgren.

Fig. 2.77 "Palm Wine Taper at the Dark Jungle" by Twihs Seven-Seven, Oshogbo, Nigeria. Collection of Juanita St. John

Fig. 2.78 Rug canvas painted in Gafsa Motifs. Designed by Ginny Ross.

Fig. 2.79 Often the strongest impetus for developing highly individual and unique forms of design grows out of a desire to do something special for someone, or for some particular place or time. Rabbit pillow designed by Elaine Magnin.

Fig. 2.80 Designed by Diane Norton, Dee Originals.

Fig. 2.81 Create a whimsical pillow or a cuddly doll for that special "little someone." "The Apple of her Eye." Designed by Ginny Ross. Stitched by Joan Heffner.

Fig. 2.82 Anniversary pillow. Designed by Elaine Magnin.

Fig. 2.83 Design a lasting family keepsake for loved ones. Beaded shoulder bag inspired by Indian lore. Designed by Gay Ann Rogers.

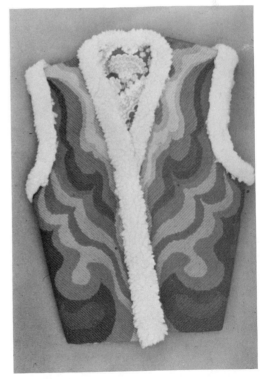

Fig. 2.84 Sherpa vest designed and worked by Ginny Ross. Brick stitch on #14 canvas. Uneven stitches were taken to accommodate the curved design.

Fig. 2.85 Give added importance to a special event or special time with the personal touch. Christmas angel by Elizabeth Bauman.

Fig. 2.86 Christmas wreath by Elaine Magnin.

Fig. 2.87 Accent your own personal lifestyle by creating a one-of-a-kind needlepoint covering for a treasured heirloom, such as the one Anne Lipscomb has done for her handsome Victorian chair, made c. 1871. The paisley pattern is adapted from a Victorian scarf by designer Gene Abel.

Can You Find
the Dimensions
3 of a Square ?

In its most literal sense, needlepoint is distinguished from other forms of embroidery by the fact that it is worked into a open-grid ground in which both warp and weft threads are evenly spaced. The precise geometric structure of this ground finds a logical extension when the applied motif is also geometric in nature. Harmony and integrity are automatically assured when ground and motif interact to support, unite, and perpetuate one another.

To most obvious method by which to form geometric shapes is through a direct confrontation with the structured grid of the ground. But as with so many other avenues of human expression, a rich vocabulary grows richer with nurturing. The more knowledge and exposure you have to geometric shape, the more varied and exciting your own interpretation of these will become.

History presents us with an almost endless well from which to draw inspiration for ideas and designs derived from geometric form. Look to other periods and other cultures and you will soon discover the fascinating pano-

Fig. 3.1 Detail of a rug, Moroccan-inspired design. Adapted by Susan Treglown.
51 Stitched by Beverly Miller.

rama of man-made forms that display the symmetrical balance, definitive order, and crisp outlines characterizing geometric patterns. Since very early times geometric design has prevailed in pattern work. Strong evidence supports the theory that these motifs were originally conceived as picture images that served to convey meaning and record information. To this very day their effectiveness as symbolic devices can be recognized in the figure of the cross, the six-pointed star, and the fleur-de-lis.

Fig. 3.2 Hagios Apostoli, Thessaloniki, Greece (10th cen.) Courtesy of Catherine Fels.

Fig. 3.3 The richly patterned brickwork observed in Byzantine architecture provides many ideas for ground and border patterns in needlework.

Fig. 3.4 The great early Indian cultures inhabiting the Americas made bold dramatic use of geometric motifs. Detail from the patio of the Palace of Columns, Milta, Oaxaca State, Mexico. (Zapotec-Mixteca architecture).

Fig. 3.5 Needlework detail adapted from patio in Fig. 3.4

By and large, however, the vast majority of geometric patterns seen today are far removed from their remote beginnings. Their original intent has been obscured as they have passed from one generation to another and have been borrowed and adapted to meet the requirements of other civilizations. Gradually the emphasis of these forms has shifted until now the importance of their form for decorative intent has superseded that of graphic content. Further, the outward appearance of their configurations has undergone alterations as they have been assimilated into a wide variety of art forms.

The basic character and intricacies that identify one craft are nonexistent in another. For example, the restrictions imposed on the stonemason precluded the making of a representation of a given pattern identical to one existing in a woven textile or wood carving. As a result, each individual art or craft has made its own special contribution to the evolution of geometric design.

Geometric design reached its zenith in the world of Islamic art. During the period in history when Muslim conquerors reigned supreme over vast reaches of central and western Asia, North Africa, and southern Europe, they carried with them an art style that was to leave an indelible imprint on the arts of man. Three basic factors shaped that style known today as Islamic art. Religious prohibitions, environmental factors, and the adaptation of established artistic traditions appropiated from subjugated lands fostered an art style that was abstract in character and depended little on representation of forms as they exist in the natural world. Instead, Islamic artists drew the substance of their inspiration from within.

It is difficult to assess the degree of indebtedness we owe to the mastery and skill with which these artisans deciphered the infinite divisions and subdivisions of the geometric module. Islamic art was essentially an art of ornamentation, and its expression was always adapted to fit the medium and the overall form of the object it was decorating. No surface was void of embellishment: small motifs were built into a central design motif compounding an ornamental surface in which there were no empty spaces.

Fig. 3.6 Detail of building facade, Milta. Photo: Frederick Mollner.

Fig. 3.7 Neelework adaptation of facade in Fig. 3.6.

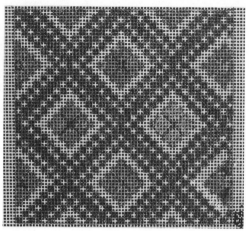

Fig. 3.8 Mayan builders used hundreds of geometrically shaped stones individually locked into place to form the magnificent mosaic facade seen on the nunnery at Uxmal.

Fig. 3.9 Needlework adapted from facade in Fig. 3.8.

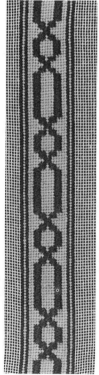

Fig. 3.10 Detail from doorway of a mosque in southern Turkey, Photo: Dr. Wachtang Djabodze.

Fig. 3.11 Needlework detail from mosque doorway.

**Can You Find
the Dimensions
of a Square**

Fig. 3.12 Japanese
sampler, 1960. Courtesy of
the Cooper-Hewitt Museum
of Decorative Arts and
Design, Smithsonian
Institution.

Fig. 3.13 Needlework table top
displaying Moroccan influence.
Designed and executed by Susan
Treglown.

Fig. 3.14 Textile fragment, Spanish (Hispana Moresque, 15th
century). Silk compound twill weave. The Nasli M. Heeramaneck
Collection, gift of Joan Palevsky. Courtesy of the Los Angeles
County Museum of Art.

Fig. 3.15 Needlework detail from fragment in Fig. 3.18.

Fig. 3.16 Needlework motif adapted from Fig. 3.18.

Fig. 3.17 One of the most enduring themes in Islamic art was the mastery with which floral motifs were interpreted through an endless progression of geometric shapes over the entire surface of a fabric. The meticulous counted work pillow cover by Irene Rosta is a beautiful example of this design style, which has been adapted to decorative textiles in many areas of the world.

Fig. 3.18 Oriental rugs provide a seemingly endless design inspiration for color and shape. Designed and executed by Irene Rosta.

56

Fig. 3.19 Detail from Fig. 3.18.

Fig. 3.20 (left) Detail from mosque. Photo:
Dr. Wachtang Djobadze.

Fig. 3.21 (right) Needlework detail
adapted from mosque.

Geometric interpretation ranged from the relatively simple to the extremely complex. Basic shapes combined with pattern to produce an art of
majestic harmony and subtle refinement splendid to both hand and eye.
In the hands of these magicians the most basic contours were interwoven
into a puzzle of complexities through the knowledgeable use of such design
devices as interlacing, overlapping, and interlocking of line and form. The
end result was design composed of shapes within shapes, endlessly traversed
by a complex maze of intersecting lines. Rhythmic integration was governed
by the principles of pattern and repetition. Within these self-imposed
limitations, Islamic artists were able to achieve infinite variety, tantalizing
intricacies, and total unity of design.

Fig. 3.22 Detail of a bas-relief in the Court of the Lions at the
Alhambra, Granada, Spain. Photo: Leonard Heath.

Fig. 3.23 Needlework adaptation from bas-relief above.

Fig. 3.24 Detail of tile work at the Alcazar, Seville, Spain. Photo: Leonard Heath.

Fig. 3.25 Patterns were borrowed and adapted from one art form to another. A Moroccan sampler dating from the 18th-19th century displays the masterful adaptation of such motifs. Courtesy of the Victoria and Albert Museum, London.

Fig. 3.26 Window detail from the entrance to the Great Mosque in Cordova, Spain. Photo: Jeanne Schnitzler.

Fig. 3.27 Needlework motif from window in Fig. 3.33.

Fig. 3.28 Looking through the grill at the Tomb of Salim, Christis, India. Photo: Lydia Takeshita.

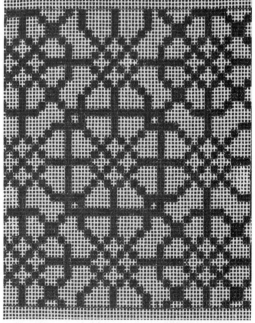

Fig. 3.29 Needlework detail based on grill in Fig. 3.35.

Fig. 3.30 The excitement generated by the infinite combinations that can evolve from geometric shapes placed on canvas continues to provoke new avenues of expression from contemporary designers as evidenced by this striking hanging titled "The Star of Yang-na" by M. Jackson Ellis, which utilizes multi-colored wools, floss, and metallic threads.

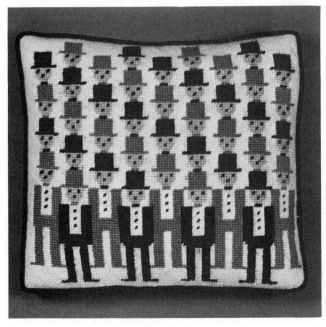

Fig. 3.31 Designer Maureen Doyle of Loretta's Needlepoint Studio uses geometric shapes with a delightful sense of humor to develop her sophisticated theme titled "Top Hats."

Decorative pulled work covers
entire surface of this bell pull
hanging designed and worked
by Ginny Ross. This type of design is best worked first on
graph paper of like size.

4 Techniques for Adapting the Design to Canvas

THE TRACING METHOD

One of the simplest methods of obtaining a design is the tracing method. Although it is not advisable to copy any original art directly, pictures of many kinds are readily adaptable. Sources for these might be coloring books, wallpaper, advertising art, large-scale illustrations, or photographs from books, magazines, newspaper, and catalogues.

This method is easy and direct. The supplies you will need are a fine-line marker; tracing, layout, or typewriter paper; and clips to fasten the copy securely. If you wish to work on a colored canvas rather than on a lined one, you will also need acrylic or oil paints and a few brushes of various sizes. If you choose to use oil paints, it will be necessary to have paint thinner to thin the paints. If you choose to use acrylic paints, it is best to thin with water.

The illustration in Figure 4-1 was traced with the fine-line marker directly from a page in a coloring book. Next, the canvas was painted with acrylic paints by placing the blank canvas on top of the tracing. If you paint carefully, it is not necessary to trace the design onto the canvas before painting.

63 Markers are used on the paper tracing but *never* on the canvas. Many

Fig. 4.1

treasured pieces of needlework have been ruined during the blocking process when marking pens labeled "permanent" have bled. In view of the fact that improvements are constantly being made, there may well be a "permanent" marker some day. If you insist on using markers, test them first (refer to information on cleaning needlepoint, page 167).

The easiest method of tracing is to use artist's tracing paper. If you use any other kind of thin paper, it will be necessary to add some kind of illumination from underneath the copy. One way this can be done is by taping the copy and the paper onto a window pane. This works well but can be very arduous if you have a great deal of tracing to do. If you are fortunate enough to have a glass-top table, all you need do is tape your copy on the underside of the top and lay your fresh paper on top of the table. If you do not have sufficient light, you can set a small lamp on the floor under the table. If you have to lay the lamp on its side, be sure to place the bulb in a foil or metal pan so that you do not cause a fire from excess heat.

If you wish to construct your own working area, you can take a pane of glass, rest it on a few books at either side, and proceed as above. If the pane of glass is rough on the edges, it is wise to protect yourself from cuts by covering all four edges with masking tape.

ENLARGEMENT

ENLARGING BY PHOTOCOPY

This is a very effective way for a novice to obtain a design of useable size. Figure 4-2 shows a flower illustration taken from a horticulture book. It

Fig. 4.2

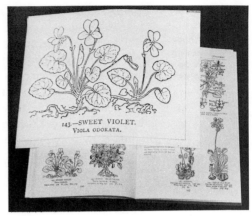

Fig. 4.3

was enlarged by photocopy process and is ready to apply to canvas. In this case the illustration used was a line drawing so it would not be necessary to trace from the photocopy onto tracing paper before applying it to canvas. This illustration would also have been very easy to enlarge by graphing (see page 66).

To make our design a bit snappier, we might add a butterfly or an insect. In this case you would look for a picture of whatever you wished to add. If you find one of the correct size, simply trace it on a piece of paper, carefully cut it out, and apply it in the correct position (see Figure 4-3).

After your pencil copy is complete, lay the design in a position such that you can stand back to look at it. If it is a pillow design, place it on a sofa or in a chair. If it is a rug, lay it on the floor. If it is a wall hanging, it is simplest to hang it from the top edge of a door using thumbtacks; this way when it is taken down no thumbtack marks will remain. With large articles, it is especially important to live with them for a few days. Sometimes they look very different the second or third time you study them.

If you are satisfied with your design after you have given it a trial, then you are ready to proceed with the transfer to canvas. If you are not satisfied, now is the time to make any change you think might improve it. Even little changes can make a big difference in the final project.

After all necessary changes have been made, trace over any pencil lines with a fine-line marker. It is easier to transfer to a piece of canvas from a black and white line drawing than it is from a pencil sketch. Be very careful that your canvas piece is positioned exactly on the square on top of your design. If you apply your design "off-square," your finished project will always be off-square (refer to Figure 4-12).

Enlargement by photocopy can normally be done by any photocopy company found in your classified telephone book. The fee is usually nominal. The transfer process is covered more fully in the section of this chapter **65** entitled "How to Paint Your Canvas" (page 71).

Techniques for Adapting the Design to Canvas

Enlargement by graph is suitable for any size project, but is especially effective for large items such as rugs and wall hangings. The most important thing to look for when considering a design for enlargement is the change of appearance. Objects do not appear the same when enlarged several times. Some people are able to visualize this; others will have to try a sample enlargement in order to decide. Flowers that are ¼ inch in diameter in the original copy may appear very dainty. If the transfer process makes them four times the copy size, they might become very cumbersome (see Figure 4-4).

An inexperienced person might find it necessary to try a sample enlargement of more than one area of a design. After you have completed your sample enlargements, look at them from a distance of several feet. In this way you will see a truer picture. If the effect is pleasing, then by all means continue. Do not spend several hours enlarging a design if you are not totally pleased with your samples.

The first step necessary in this method of enlargement is to mark off the design to be copied in squares. Each one of these squares will be transferred to the corresponding square of your enlargement. If you wish to enlarge something 4 times, your small design would be marked off in ¼-inch grid lines and your large copy would be marked off in one-inch grid lines. Figure 4-5 shows a partially completed enlargement.

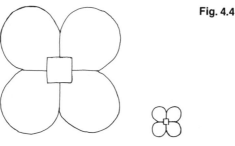

Fig. 4.4

Fig. 4.5

This illustration was based on two times enlargement. This is a relatively simple enlargement. The same is true of four times enlargment. If you wish to enlarge five, six, seven, or eight times, it is much wiser to purchase transparent graph paper. This is available in many needlepoint stores. It is also possible to purchase 36-inch wide paper marked off in 1-inch grids.

If you are going to make your own grid guide, use transparent paper or acetate. Mark off your lines very accurately with black ink. Now mark off a sheet of large white paper with one-inch grid lines using pencil. If you use pencil on your grid lines, it is a simple task to erase all these lines after you have completed the transfer process. It will also be much easier to do your final painting if the grid lines have been removed.

The rest of the enlargement process is quite easy but it is time-consuming. You must transfer all the lines that appear in the original small design to each corresponding square of your large copy. You do not have to be an artist to do this but you do have to be accurate.

Fig. 4.6 This 3′ × 5′ rug was designed and executed by Ginny Ross. The stylized figures were taken from manuscripts dating from the Byzantine period.

Fig. 4.7 This handsome tiger would be a welcome addition to any type of decor. Designed by Nina, New York City.

Techniques for Adapting the Design to Canvas

Decoupage is the art of cutting out and pasting; hence the name given to this process. Basically, it is what its name implies: Cut-out shapes are arranged on a blank surface forming a new design. It is usually possible to find various elements for decoupage all in correct proportion. If, however, you find the right picture but its size is wrong, it is quite easy either to enlarge or decrease the measurements of any object you wish to use in your design.

Decoupage is a very desirable process for a beginner. It allows for many mistakes, and also allows the inexperienced person to see different arrangements before the actual transfer process is started. This cut-out process can be extended to almost any kind of design. One could gather flower pictures from various sources, for instance, arranging them until a pleasant composition appeared. This is the most satisfactory method for a novice to use in the designing of any rather large project.

If you have a variety of different elements in your design, you will have to tape them all in position. It is best to make one final clear tracing of your paste-up before transferring the design to canvas.

TRANSFERRING A DESIGN TO GRAPH PAPER

Designs can be classified as geometric or nongeometric. Geometrics establish a totally countable pattern; nongeometrics can be completely free-flowing.

Geometrics are the simplest designs to transfer to graph paper. It is merely a matter of accurate counting. Graph paper can be obtained in most sizes from drafting supply houses, and now transparent graph paper can be obtained in many needlepoint shops. If you cannot obtain the identical scale number graph paper you wish, it is not an insurmountable problem. The Victorian house in Figure 2-2 was graphed on no. 10 paper and stitched on no. 14 canvas.

When using differently sized mesh and paper, you must be aware of the total size change. No. 14 canvas (14 stitches to the inch) will stitch to 1⅜ inches on no. 10 canvas. Simply divide the total number of graph squares by the size number of the canvas (no. 10, no. 12, etc.) you wish to use. For example, if you had a design on no. 10 graph paper and the total width was 112 squares (11-plus inches), then

$$\frac{8 \text{ inches on no. 14 canvas}}{14 \,\overline{\smash{\big)}\,112}}$$

If you have a free-flowing design and you wish to work from a graph, transfer must take place from a sketch of like size. Your first step would be enlargement by one of the methods described in this book.

You would then outline the design on your sketch with a black marker. Center this under your graph paper, fastening the two together. Lightly trace with pencil. Refine your design by coding individual squares for color change.

Fig. 4.8   The United Nations Peace Rug consists of 140 squares of flawlessly executed basketweave stitch. Individual coats of arms are assembled in alphabetical order with the United Nations seal in the center of the rug. The rug was accepted by Kurt Waldheim, Secretary-General, in ceremonies held on October 23, 1975, and is now permanently displayed in the visitors' lobby. This outstanding piece of needlework was designed by Mona Spoor and was stitched by 35 outstanding craftsmen, all members of the American Needlepoint Guild. Each square is 16 inches in width and is worked on #16 mesh.

Photo: C.L. Crenshaw.

If you are graphing for a single-count stitch, use 1 square for each stitch. Use 2 squares by 2 squares for any regular cross stitch. If you are graphing for Florentine embroidery, use 4 squares (or 2, 6, or 8 squares) by 1 square. Stitch count is very important when you are applying stitches to graph paper (see Figure 4-9).

Fig. 4.9 Peter Ashe, San Francisco designer, captures the charm of the Victorian period of elegance in this highly geometric picture. Notice the attention given to such small details as the front door glass.

Fig. 4.10 Two handsome designs are achieved by Elaine Magnin by effectively combining graphic letters and shadow technique.

Fig. 4.11 When executing designs that must be completely symmetrical, it is always necessary to count your stitches. Both of these dolls were counted during the stitching process. Patchwork doll designed and stitched by Ginny Ross. Victorian doll designed by Elizabeth Bauman and stitched by Judy Peters.

HOW TO PAINT A CANVAS

Painting the canvas is an extremely important step in the design process. The supplies you will need are various acrylic or oil paints, a few brushes, and a mixing pan. If you are going to use oil paints, you will also need some turpentine or cigarette lighter fluid to thin the paints. Lighter fluid speeds the drying process. Acrylics are thinned with water.

You will need at least one ¼-inch flat brush and one small pointed brush for detail. It is easiest to have a selection of several sizes, but brushes are quite expensive and it is possible to paint adequately with just the two sizes. Canvas is very hard on brushes, so do not select the most costly brand.

Since all colors can be mixed from various combinations of the three primary colors, the minimum purchase of paint would be three tubes, one each of red, yellow, and blue. Again, you will find it more convenient to have a selection of various colors plus black and white. The best solution for a mixing pan is an empty plastic egg carton. The small cups are ideally suited for mixing small amounts of paint.

Begin by placing your prepared line drawing under your prepared piece of canvas. Place these two items on your work surface, which you will already have protected with newspaper or wrapping paper. You may use either masking tape or thumbtacks to secure your sketch and canvas in place.

Attach each piece individually, one on top of the other, to the newspaper surface. If you think it would be more satisfactory to paint on a slanted surface, then you will have to insert a piece of wood. For this it is possible to buy a drawing board from an art supply store or a 24-inch square piece of plywood from any home improvement store. You can even use your breadboard. If you use your breadboard, take extra care to use sufficient newspaper to protect the sketch from any oil which might be on the surface of the board. You may use anything to elevate the edge farthest away from the edge of the table. Using one or two books work very well.

Attach the canvas only on the top and on one side. The other two sides are left open so you can lift up your canvas in case you need to clarify some area of your sketch.

Use two empty jars for cleaning water. One jar should be used for light colors and the other for dark colors. Paint should be thinned to the consistency of cream. Mix a few of the colors you know you will need. There is no real rule as to where you start painting; however, if there is any area that requires counting in order to obtain uniformity, then it would be wise to paint that first. Some people paint from the center out. Others find it more convenient to paint subjects of like colors at the same time. You will find a preference after you have experimented.

Above all, try to be neat and precise. The better your canvas is painted, the easier you will find it to stitch. If you make any marks that you wish to cover, do so with white acrylic paint. Even a small dark spot will show through a white or light background yarn.

It is usually not necessary to mark a solid line at the perimeter of your design. If you do find it necessary, use a pale blue or pale yellow to mark the line; do not use black. It is usually adequate to indicate just the four corners.

Many stores sell ink markers for use on needlepoint canvas. Beware of them. They may say that they are permanent, but that does not necessarily mean that they are. If you insist on using some brand of marker, test it several times before you use it. Make several marks on a scrap of canvas. Let it dry and then soak it in water to see if the colors run. Remember that anything you put on your canvas during the preparation process must stay permanent during the wet blocking process described later in this book. An additional precaution can be the application of one of the spray fixatives available in art supply stores. This is not necessary if a reputable brand of acrylic or oil paints has been used.

Acrylic paints will dry almost instantly while oil paints can take several days to dry. Stitching can begin immediately after the paints are dry.

Before you begin the painting process, be doubly sure that you have your sketch positioned directly on the square of the canvas. If your design has been applied slightly off-square, it will remain off during the life of the article. This will also cause problems during the mounting process.

Fig. 4.12 Off-square design.

Fig. 4.13 A symmetrical balance of this graceful floral is emphasized by its octagonal shape. Designed by Candi Martin, Candamar Designs.

PLANNING FOR A RUG

Doing a needlepoint rug is a monumental project. Of course, size is totally relative. A 3-by-5-foot rug may be considered a giant undertaking to one person, yet to another it may be considered a medium-sized project. In any event, it is not wise to start a rug of any size until you are fairly confident of your ability and very knowledgeable about your limitations. If putting off the start of a rug until you have completed one more project would help your confidence, then by all means do that. Most all of the problems you will encounter in doing a rug will come to light in the course of doing about four or five smaller articles. By that time your confidence should be firm enough for you to begin a rug.

One of the prime prerequisites for starting a rug of any size is the desire to make one. Making a rug is not like making a pillow; it is bulky in your hands and sometimes heavy on your lap. But it is probably the most singularly rewarding thing that you could ever make. Just remember that a rug which measures 3 feet by 5 feet has the same total number of square inches as fifteen 12-inch pillows!

Designing a rug can be a awesome task; all elements must be in total proportion. If your artistic ability is limited, the only choice you may have is to use one of the enlargement methods described in this book. Certainly buying a painted canvas from a store is possible, but in recent years the cost of a hand-painted rug canvas has become great and is not possible given **73** budgets of the majority of needlepointers (see Figure 4-14).

Fig. 4.14   English ribbon floral artistically executed by Rosalie
Peters, Sharianne Designs. Photo: Art Kantor.

It is very foolish to embark on a rug just for the sake of doing a rug. If the
design is not good or the subject matter is not exactly what you would like it
to be, then do not begin. You must be enthused or you will soon lose interest and your rug will be relegated to your hall closet. Yarn cost and the time
necessary will be the same whether you are doing a bad design or a good
design. There are several good rug design books now in publication for use
by a "nonartistic" person.

No matter how you approach a rug, it is extremely important for you to
do a critique before you begin stitching. Lay your design on the floor . . .
stand back . . . look . . . even live with it for a few days to see if anything
comes to mind that displeases you. If all is well after a few days, then
proceed.

The painting process is the same as for smaller things, with one exception:
You must have a large area upon which to work. The dining room table
works well. Be sure to protect the surface of your table with newspaper.
Cover this newspaper with the white paper upon which you have drawn
your design. Now firmly attach your canvas to your paper pattern. Your
working surface must be large enough to accomodate the full size of your
project. The design pattern will slip if it is not firmly attached to your
canvas in a flat position. It is also possible to work on the floor, but it is
usually uncomfortable and rather difficult to paint easily.

Allow yourself a great deal of time for painting. At this point, you should
know how long it takes you to paint an average pillow design. It could con-
ceivably take 30 to 40 hours to complete the painting of a rug.

There are four basic stitches that are satisfactory for making a rug. They
are the half-cross trame stitch; the smyrna cross stitch; the basic Florentine
work known as Bargello; and basketweave stitch. The half-cross trame and

smyrna cross stitches are good only for fairly geometric designs such as the Mondrian-inspired pillow shown in illustration 2-73. They do not work well with most needlepoint designs. Bargello is a rather different approach. Design can be achieved through change of color rather than through figured, painted design. Color plate 17 shows a rug worked in nine-ply Persian yarn on no. 5 canvas. Basketweave is the most satisfactory stitch and can readily be used on any design. This stitch is used in color plate 30. Basketweave does not distort too greatly and the stitching process is easy to handle, starting from any given corner and always working down. This allows the stitched area to fall away in front of you and you are never in a position where your hand must hold worked needlepoint. DO NOT EVER USE CONTINENTAL STITCH IN MAKING A RUG. The distortion is so great in a large project that the chances of ever keeping it square are very small.

While it is possible to use a frame, it is much more enjoyable not to use one. Several reasons are given in the section covering frames (see page 108). The largest realistic size to make without piecing is 4 feet by 6 feet. When planning a rug to be made in sections, extreme care must be taken to make sure that all the pieces are accurately counted with equal number of stitches on matching sections. The design must also be planned very carefully. It is advisable to place seams in such a way that they are camouflaged, either by a change of color or a change of design. See Chapter X.

5 The Excitement of Color

Color is one of the first elements in a piece of needlepoint to awaken an immediate response on both a conscious and a subconscious level. Its presence generates excitement, determines the character of the design, and structures both mood and depth in every design. Each stitch taken by the needlepointer, regardless of subject matter or hue, utilizes color in tangible form to build substance.

Of all the design elements, color is also the most flexible. Its selection and control on the part of each individual is a very personal thing. For this reason the kind and quality of color selected for a given work will be governed largely by personal taste, the predetermined purpose and placement of the article, and the skillful interpretation of color fundamentals as they relate to that project. With each work undertaken, function and taste may vary, but the inherent properties and dimensions of color apply in general to all designs. Understanding these fundamentals will provide greater flexibility and effectiveness in needlepoint design.

Fig. 5.1 Color wheel.

Volumes can and have been written about color, but the best way to know and understand it is by experimenting with color yourself. Start by observing the relationships of the color hues to one another on the color wheel. The most basic color system is formulated on the three primary hues—yellow, red, and blue. These colors are termed *primary* because they are the parents from which all other hues on the wheel are made.

By combining equal parts of pairs of these primary hues, the *secondary* hues—orange, violet, and green—result. A third color division takes place when the primary hues are mixed with adjacent secondary hues to create the *intermediary* hues—yellow-orange, red-orange, red-violet, blue-violet, blue-green, and yellow-green (Figure 5-2).

Viewing the color sequence on the wheel, we can see at a glance how all of the hues flow into one another to approximate the color spectrum. Based on the natural order of radiant energies, the spectrum exists in a state of perfect color balance. Good color in design utilizes this principle of energy balance to satisfy our innate psychological, physiological, and aesthetic needs. For this reason color schemes composed of pure hues are most successful when each of the primary areas of the light spectrum is represented in some way (see Figure 5-3).

All hues represented on the color wheel are considered to be in a pure or nearly pure state and of equal intesity. The use of pure hues is very evident in all aspects of contemporary art; however, it is often desirable and even

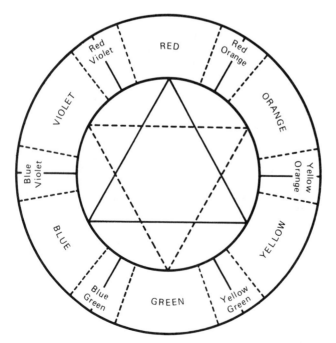

Fig. 5.2   The three primary areas of the spectrum.

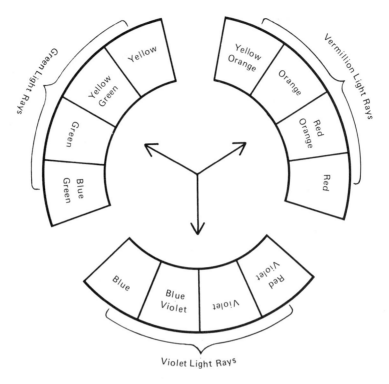

Fig. 5.3 Color triads.

necessary to use color that has been modified in some way. This modification is best achieved when four factors of color selection and control are taken into consideration: color properties, color qualities, color harmonies, and color functions.

COLOR PROPERTIES

HUE

Hue is the term used to identify a given color and at the same time define its relative degree of purity. For example, *the hue yellow* means pure yellow which has not been modified in any way.

INTENSITY

Pure hues are more intense than color that has been mixed. Evaluating a hue in terms of its intensity refers to noting its brightness or dullness, and its degree of neutrality. Colors of high intensity, such as red and orange, are very close to pure hues. Colors such as pastel pink, light blue, and beige are colors of low intensity.

Value is another factor inherent in all color. The value of a color defines its properties of lightness or darkness. Every known hue has a range of values that spans gradations from nearly white to nearly black. Light color values result when white is added to a pure hue to produce a *tint*. Pastel pink, pale green, and lavender are examples of tints. Pure colors with the addition of black are called *shades*. Maroon and forest green are shades of red and green, respectively. When both black and white (i.e., gray) are added to pure color, a *color tone* results. Dusty rose is a color tone.

CHROMA

Chroma is the term used to designate any color in which some quality of hue can be identified. Olive green, rust brown, and mustard yellow are examples of chromatic colors. *Achromatic* colors are those colors devoid of chroma, referred to as neutrals. Black, white, and gray are neutral colors.

COLOR QUALITIES

In addition to the physical properties of color, all color is classified as either warm or cool. Warm colors, such as red, orange, and magenta have high frequency in long wave lengths. By psychological response we associate these colors with warm things, such as fire and sunlight. In a composition warm colors stimulate. They make objects advance and expand. When large areas of vivid warm color are placed next to one another, they tend to cancel one another. Generally bright warm color is most effective when used in measured quantities. Cool colors, such as blue, green, and turquoise, have short wave lengths. They make objects and shapes tend to recede and contract. By psychological conditioning they wake feelings of relaxation and calm. We identify cool colors with cool things, such as water, grass, and ice.

This information is very useful for developing a composition. Because muted colors make objects and shapes appear more distant and less conspicuous, they act as a foil to activate and contrast with areas of warm, brilliant color. The warm and cool qualities of color should always be considered in addition to the color properties in establishing color balance.

COLOR HARMONY

Unrelated hues skillfully modified in intensity and value can combine to form harmonious relationships. Color harmony is also achieved when combinations of colors related by hue are used. The following color schemes provide a basic guide to color relationships.

Monochromatic is the term used to describe the use of various intensities of shades, tints, and tones possible in any given hue.

Complementary color schemes employ colors located opposite one another on the color wheel. Red and green, violet and yellow, and blue and orange are a few of the color combinations that form complementary color schemes.

Analogous color schemes comprise any series of hues located adjacent to one another on the color wheel. Because of their close proximity to each other, analogous color is always related and provides a safe basis for building a color scheme.

Black, white, gray, beige, and brown are considered *neutral* colors. A neutral color scheme is made up of two or more neutral colors. Neutral color schemes can be quite dramatic when the extremes of light and dark are employed.

Other color combinations include the triads, tetrads, and split complements. Any three hues located equidistant on the color wheel will form a *triad*. All major areas of the color spectrum are found in this kind of color scheme in representational balance. Red, yellow, and blue form the primary triad. Orange, violet, and green form the secondary triad. The intermediary color can also be used in a triad: Yellow-orange, red-violet, and blue-green, or blue-violet, yellow-green, and red-orange form color combinations that compose triads.

Fig. 5.4 Color tetrads.

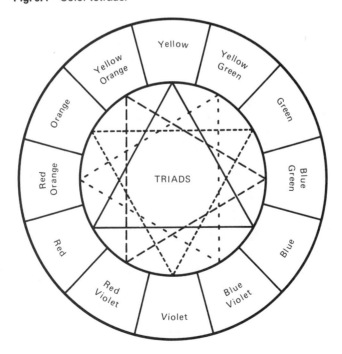

A color scheme combining any four hues located an equal distance from one another on the color wheel form a *tetrad*. Yellow-orange, red, blue-violet, and green make up a tetrad. (color plate 1).

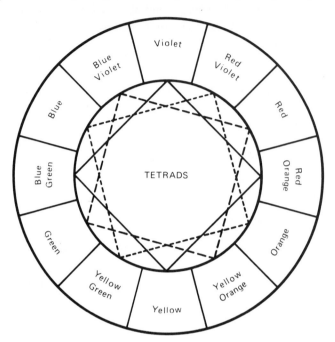

Fig. 5.5 Split complementaries.

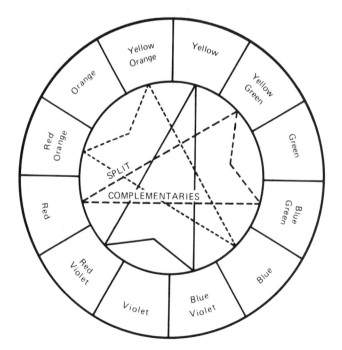

The *split complement* offers a very sophisticated and rhythmic plan. Split complements result when one hue is selected and used in combination with the two hues located on either side of its direct complement. Red, yellow-green, and blue-green; and blue, red-orange, and yellow-orange are color combinations that form split complements.

Strict adherence to any one of the basic color schemes does not assure creative expression. Creative art has no formula. Color schemes are most meaningful when they serve as a guide for further individual color exploration. The intangible ingredients provided by individual interpretation and the mark of the selective eye imbue color in design with its greatest interest and vitality.

THE FUNCTIONS OF COLOR

The multifaceted nature of color speaks a language of its own. On impact it can lure or dazzle; distort or define; calm or provoke. When skillfully manipulated, color adds depth and dimension to thematic interpretation. Subject matter translated directly from nature is given clarification and emphasis through color.

Color has the power to capture a mood. Personal emotions and inner feelings can be projected in potent terms through color dynamics and color association. Anger, melancholy, quiescence, joy, or loneliness can all find counterparts in color.

Color is symbolic. The riotous mélange of red, yellows, warm browns, and vibrant oranges are synonomous with autumn. Soft, watery pastels reflect the delicacy and refinement associated with the Rococo period, while rich, deep reds, blues, and yellows characterize the glorious hues found in the stained-glass windows, illuminated manuscripts, and Gothic paintings of the Middle Ages.

In a more academic sense color is a tool. Selective repetition of color can develop and control rhythm and unity in a given work. A single hue repeated in several areas of a composition aids balance, directs the reading pattern, and collects shapes.

Each color used interacts with adjacent color by activating or subduing it. Warm hues appear warmer when juxtaposed with cool hues. Neutralized or grayed tones placed next to smaller areas of pure hues create in the latter the illusion of luminescence. Opposite hues of high intensity set up vibrations when used in combination.

Consider your color selections in terms of the amount you will use. Dark grounds tend to absorb light and heighten the quality of brightness in pure hues. Light hue interspersed with pure hues make the latter look richer. The extremes of light and dark are black and white. Both of these colors should be used with great care by the needlepointer. Large areas of black tend to be harsh and overpowering. Black outlines tend to be heavy and often ''jump out,'' or isolate shapes. Dark blues, greens, and browns will often provide adequate delineation while affecting a softer appearance.

White added in small amounts gives freshness, sparkle, and vitality to adjacent color. When used in large amounts its intense light concentration may easily dominate a composition and render other color less effective. Yellow changes character easily. Artificial light often causes it to fade or disappear. This is an important factor to consider when selecting yellow yarns for use in large quantities on interior pieces.

Interesting contrasts and appropriateness should be primary factors in any color selection. Seek variation in a color range and some comparisons from bright to dull, light to dark, and warm to cool. Too much sameness in color produces monotony; too much variation chaos.

Be aware that the concentrated hanks of brightly colored yarns seen in daylight at a shop will appear somewhat different when worked into canvas. The soft textures of needlepoint wools absorb light. All color mellows when worked. Further, yarn color will be affected by the textures of the stitch used. Pile or high-rise stitches modulate light and shadow, giving the illusion of deeper, more intense color. Flat stitches tone down the color, making it appear slightly darker.

SHADING

Many kinds of designs are enhanced by shading. The technique of shading may be attempted with varying degrees of complexity, from the relatively simple to the very complex. Subject matter and the size of the object or objects within the dimensions of the design will determine the degree of shading necessary and possible.

In the most basic approach several shades and tints of one color can be used for modeling. Color toward the center of an object is lighter and brighter with progressively darker gradations of shades worked toward the outer edges. Designs employing the concept of realistic perspective are developed on the same principle. In the foreground colors are lighter and brighter, grading to darker, duller color as objects recede into the distance.

To give the impression of dimension to predominant objects it is not always necessary to use each degree of gradation found within a single hue on the color chart; instead you can skip every other tone. Intricate compositions, such as landscapes, may require more gradual shading, and this is best achieved with a consecutive selection of tones.

Shaded color should be applied in uneven lines, never in bands. Shadow contours are more convincing when worked in soft contours where the corner stitch has been left out.

A no. 14 canvas worked in two-ply yarn is generally recommended for subject matter which is shaded. Complex shading is best facilitated by no. 18 canvas with one-ply yarn. For very traditional techniques approximating tapestry you may even wish to separate two strands of yarn and then mix them together, by twisting them, to achieve the required nuances of color.

Plate 1 Basic color wheel, Paternayan wool, 3-ply.

The magnificent display of color in nature remains unsurpassed and provides us with an unending source from which to gain inspiration for exciting and unique color combinations.
From a mere handful of examples we can observe . . .

Plate 2 Vibrant color contrasts: autumn leaves. Photo: Stanley G. Pateman.

Plate 3 Luminous incandescence: chrysalis. Photo: Frederick Mollner.

Plate 4 Iridescent shimmer: a peacock feather. Photo: Frederick Mollner.

Plate 5 Dramatic use of neutrals: a moth. Photo: Frederick Mollner.

Plate 6 Subtleties of color gradation: a single rose petal. Photo: Frederick Mollner.

Plate 7 Petit point purse. Traditional needlepoint, often referred to as "needle tapestry," used small uniform petit point stitches, narrative themes, and complex color gradations and shading. Courtesy of the Los Angeles County Museum of Art.

Many contemporary art movements use theories of color energy and spatial relationships to create optical illusions. The two needlework pieces [right, below] employ these concepts.

Plate 8 "Four Square." Designed by Jeanne Schnitzler. Stitched by Ginger Gardner.

Plate 9 Adaptation of a Victor Vaserly. Designed by Susan Treglown. Collection of Eadie Kleiman

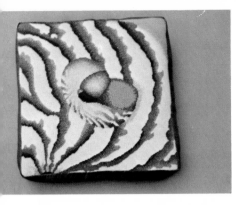

Plate 10 Greatly enlarged details of the center motif shell cover the background of this pillow design by Bettie Bearden, Papillon.

Plate 11 Two elaborate needlework panels flank a corresponding stained glass window to form the work title "The Peaceable Kingdom." Designed by Judson Studios.

Plate 13 Detail from "The Peaceable Kingdom."

Plate 12 "The Peaceable Kingdom" displays extremely rich textures and elegant rhythms from the select application and variety of stitches.

Plate 14 "Mudejar." 12′ × 15′ rug worked in adaptations of Bargello stitches. Wool on canvas. Designed by Jeanne Schnitzler.

Plate 16 Needlepoint dinner jacket done in a paisley pattern. Designed by Gene Abel for John Cook. Stitched by Anne Lipscomb on #24 canvas.

Plate 15 Fur-trimmed Florentine embroidered coat designed by Wendy Bellamy, Saint Martin's School of Art. Photo: Graham Murrell, United Kingdom.

Plate 17 Several different moods are expressed in this selection of tennis items. Racquet at left is an adaptation of a Vaserly painting as designed by Bettie Bearden, Papillon. "Les India" design is by Jebba Needlepoint, Corona del Mar. Intricate Imari design is by Ginny Ross. Tarten cover was worked in diagonal plaid stitch. Tennis shoes were designed by Candis Ipswitch.

Plate 18 Three lovely spring florals were designed by Candi Martin, Candamar Designs.

Plate 20 Dee Norton designed these two realistic animal pillows. Notice the tail which has been added to the donkey. Both pillows stitched by Natalie Howard. Photo: Michael St. John.

Plate 19 These three-dimensional stuffed animals are right at home in their forest setting. Added dimension has been given to the raccoon and the frog by using various stitches. Round shape of the turtle was obtained by wet blocking over a bowl. Raccoon and frog designed by Chottie Alderson and stitched by Natalie Howard. Turtle designed by Ginny Ross, stitched by Mary Lue Hannah.

Plate 21 Elegant elephant design by DeDe Ogden uses vibrant color and intricate stitch detail.

Plate 23 Stylized calico cat design by DeDe Ogden is a superb blending of color, texture, and design.

Plate 22 Harmonious blending of theme and design is executed on these four Christmas stockings. *Santa* and *Angel with Horn* were designed by Mayo. *Tom* and *Claire* (designed by Harriet Herdering, Mitoma Enterprises) were stitched by Toni Gray and Harriet Hendering.

Plate 24 Chiffon dress with needle work bodice designed by Jeanne Schnitzler. Needlework bodice stitched by Rosemary Ward on #14 canvas with DMC.

Plate 25 Detail of 24.

Plate 26 Delicate French floral was stitched on #18 canvas by Dorothy Tuohy. Designed by Ginny Ross.

Plate 27 This handsome geometric pillow was designed and stitched by Judy Hunt. Various stitches were first graphed on paper and then transferred to canvas.

Plate 28 Endless design ideas are found in various ethnic cultures. Indian lore inspired both of these designs by [l] Gay Ann Rogers and [r] Lee Stanley, Lass Designs.

Plate 29 This handsome stylized tulip pillow is one of the many beautiful designs executed by Jebba.

Plate 30 This study in line graphically illustrates harmonious blending of color and design. Design was worked in fern stitch. Designed by Ginny Ross.

Plate 31 This contemporary Persian paisley design by Ginny Ross is executed in brilliant colors. The three stages of a project are shown: sketch, painted canvas, and stitched work.

Plate 32 Sassy calico cat pillow by Lee Stanley of Lass Designs rests happily on area rug stitched by Terry Carver. Ancient Spanish tile work inspired this four-corner repeat design by Ginny Ross.

Plate 33 Outstanding picture of a spring basket of flowers utilizes pulled yarn stitches. Ground has been covered by a skip-bargello pattern leaving equal areas open and covered. This open-ground method adds great depth to the work. Designed by and stitched by Ginny Ross.

85

The Excitement of Color

Attainment of a knowledgeable and innovative handling of color could easily be one of the most interesting and rewarding aspects of your adventures in needlework. The tremendous range and variety of color found in present-day needlework yarns present an almost limitless panorama from which to create and enhance visual excitement in needlework design.

6 Texture

Texture stimulates two sensory responses simultaneously: by stimulating our sense of sight, texture identifies and characterizes specific objects and images; by activating our sense of touch, visual reality is clarified and heightened by tactile response.

Man's acute awareness of nature's vast source of textural enrichment, combined with a conviction to expose and explore the characteristics of substances from which we create, have resulted in the production of an amazing array of textures in everyday surroundings. Contemporary arts and crafts also reflect a strong preoccupation with textural effects. Yet it is interesting to note that the textural explosion present in most other art forms has been noticeably restrained in canvaswork.

Fig. 6.1 Every period of needlework displays the use of texture in its own distinctive way. Great emphasis has been placed on the combination of stitches and materials used to develop this needlework panel dating from 1850-1890 (wool, silk, chenille, and cut beads on canvas). Gift of the estate of Mrs. Emily M.P. Forbes. Courtesy of the Los Angeles County Museum of Art.

Fig. 6.2 Photo: Frederick Mollner.

Fig. 6.3 Photo: Don Urquidi.

Fig. 6.4 Photo: Paul Hansen.

Fig. 6.5 Neckpiece of sterling silver, copper, and quartz. Designer and craftswoman Carolyn Rosser.

Fig. 6.6 Wood sculpture, "73 People" by Leonard Heath.

Fig. 6.7 Linecut "Bust of a Woman (After Cranach the Younger)" by Pablo Picasso, 1958. Norton Simon, Los Angeles.

Fig. 6.8 Silk and metallic threads are worked into a rich collection of patterns and stitches in this magnificent 14th-century Italian Ophrey. Costume Council Fund, 1972. Courtesy of the Los Angeles County Museum of Art.

Fig. 6.9 Needlework hanging designed by Mayo. Stitched by Mickey Erichenhofer.

Fig. 6.10 Contemporary sculptured area rug designed and executed by Jeanne Schnitzler.

Fig. 6.11 Minute chain stitches worked in silk were combined with beads and gold bullion on a 60-count French gauze ground to form the decorative surface of an evening bag dating from 1890. Courtesy of Ginny Ross.

For many years skill and craftsmanship in needlework has been measured by a standard that has fostered surfaces displaying a uniformity of stitches and yarns worked into the canvas ground with machine-like precision. This concept was introduced late in the history of needlework. We have only to view the masterful embroideries and canvaswork of the 14th, 15th, and 16th centuries to realize that much of their beauty and richness was derived from their characteristic surface variations. These variations came about from a selective mixture of threads and the uneven quality of the handspun **90** worsteds employed.

Fig. 6.12   The subtle changes in stitches enrich the elegantly
patterned surface of this Persian embroidered evening bag
dating from the 16th century. Gift of Miss Estelle Levy,
Courtesy of the Los Angeles County Museum of Art.

Ironically, preconceived textural limitations in needlepoint also bear strong opposition to the nature of the medium itself. Each design, regardless of subject matter or purpose, is composed from a series of individual stitches. Texture is an automatic outgrowth of the technique. With this in mind, it remains for the craftsman to decide how much and what kind of texture will best support and enhance the design at hand.

Designs making use of complex subject matter and a variety of color, shapes, and details usually depend upon subtle textures and uniformity of techniques to maintain their continuity. Uneven surfaces tend to weaken, distort, and even obscure the existing elements in this type of design. On the other hand, simple designs often gain increased vitality and expression through the addition of deliberate textural enrichment.

In all needlework, color, texture, and light are interdependent upon one another. Light reveals texture by identifying differences in stitches and threads. Color takes on tonal variation when surface changes occur. Dark color look darker when seen in shadow, and light color become lighter and brighter when light strikes the high point of its exterior. In essence, texture sets up a theme of contrasts based on the interaction of light and shadow. Further elaboration takes place when there are tactile differences in the materials and these materials alter structural relationships. By manipulating these factors, there are many ways in which texture can be emphasized and expanded.

Fig. 6.13 Overall view of Fig. 6-12.

Fig. 6.14 French knots create an explosion of flowers in the needlework composition *Flower Stall* by designer Peter Ashe.

The most obvious method for developing structural differences is through the stitches themselves. Each stitch makes its own kind of texture. For this reason interest in composition does not depend on using a wide variety of stitches, but it does depend on using a selective number of stitches which will give maximum variety and contrast. Change the length, the direction, and the nature of the line in your stitches. Texture will then be developed from the twists and turns in each stitch. Use grainy stitches, such as the smyrna cross stitch, the French knot, or knotted threads to grab light and set up an area of rhythmic staccato. Use the surface shadows cast from high-rise stitches to add depth and a whole collection of new shapes. Intensify tactile sensations by using cut, looped, tufted, or plaited threads.

Seek out the rich textural effects incorporated in pattern. Pattern compounds textures and at the same time arranges them into a repetitive tempo. This syncopated measure offers the craftsman a regulating device for controlling the exact amount of texture desired, and at the same time, it challenges each individual to experiment with a fresh, new interpretation. An innovative progression of pattern can generate enough decorative excitement to form an entire work.

Create unique textures through a discriminating selection of materials. Fibers are a primary source of both texture and design inspiration in all areas of the textile arts. Today the selection of fibers is so wide that it suggests a new dimension in 20th-century needlework. Every material contains its own distinctive character to arouse a creative response.

Texture   Traditionally, wool has been used for needlepoint. Soft, warm, and pliable, it is the nature of its fiber to accept dyestuffs readily, providing a vast range of color for many different kinds of designs.

Silk is a fiber that has been renowned in all forms of needlework since the days of antiquity. Treasured for its luxurious texture and lustrous sheen, silk is also an exceptionally strong and durable fiber. By itself, silk produces a delicate surface alive with shimmering lights. When mixed with other fibers, silk will bring added highlights, color depth, and luminous surface qualities.

Metallics give sparkle and concentrate light reflections, while fine, twisted linen looks dull and smooth when worked into the canvas. Like wool, linen can be obtained in a variety of weights and is often identified by rough slubs and novelty twists.

Rayon, nylon, and other manmade fibers should not be overlooked. Many of these materials offer artistic potential at a more nominal cost than do natural fibers. It is important, however, to examine their physical properties from the standpoint of durability, flexibility, and dye stability. Some synthetics are easily damaged by harsh light, heavy wear, or climatic changes.

Consider your choice of materials in terms of weight and scale. Thick yarns used in combination with thinner yarns will not only create differences in the look and feel of your design, but may also alter the scale of the different design elements to one another. Thin, tightly twisted fibers project refinement. Thick, coarse, or uneven fibers produce weightiness and tend to emphasize an earthy quality.

Investigation is one of the key factors to the successful development of needlepoint texture. Don't be afraid to try something different or use an old idea in a new way. A few guidelines will aid in deciding what kinds of textures might be most effective in the design at hand. Always be aware that texture gains impact from contrast. Reinforce the importance of smooth yarns or stitches by placing them next to rough or undulating surfaces. Dramatize changes in spacial dimensions by putting the highest areas next to the lowest ones. Textures located at a distance from one another do not command the immediate attention that adjacent textures do.

This knowledge can be used in reverse. Striking textural effects can be gained from deliberate understatement. Subtle nuances of textural change often endow a work with surface intricacies that tantalize and hold attention for long periods of time. The longer you look, the more interesting and exciting the work becomes.

Choose textures carefully so they will act as a tool to give your design both contrast and harmony. At worst, your texture will be inventive and overdone. At best, it will create decorative enrichment and sensitive articulation for the existing surface.

Jacobean leaves are skillfully entwined to cover the surface of
this rug designed by Ginny Ross

7 Starting Out Right

HOW TO BUY CANVAS

Canvas is the name given to the woven fabric base upon which one stitches. It is also know as *scrim.* Colors range from white to beige and even to dull green. As far as a person's eyes are concerned, white canvas is the easiest to use; however, in many instances white is not the most suitable color.

Most canvas is imported into the United States, but canvas is now being produced domestically. Its fiber content is either cotton, linen, or occasionally hemp. Various manufacturers use different substances for the sizing. This accounts for the wide range of canvas texture, which spans all the way from ultrasmooth to extremely rough.

Mesh size begins at a tiny twenty-four holes to the inch to a very large 3 holes to the inch. Always remember that the larger the number canvas the smaller the holes will be. Widths also vary greatly. Some canvas is as narrow as 18 inches, and rug canvas is 60 inches wide. All canvas is either *mono,* (with single grid) (plain or interlocking) or *penelope* (with double grids). Figure 7-1 illustrates the difference.

95

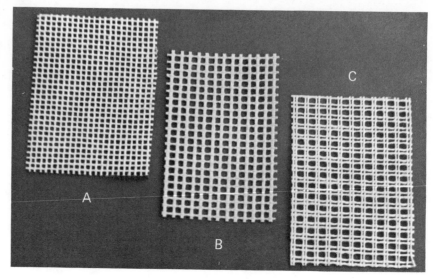

Fig. 7.1 A: Plain mono; B: Interlocking mono; C: Penelope.

Mono canvas is an excellent all-around serviceable canvas. It can be obtained in two styles, either plain or interlocking. Both kinds have their good points and their bad points. Plain mono is the *only* canvas to use if you ever expect to do flawless, effortless basketweave stitch. If you continue needlepoint past the "casual try" stage, it is certain that you will want to use this kind of canvas and basketweave stitch. The reasons behind this statement are covered in the section on basketweave stitch (see page 124). Interlocking canvas is just what the name implies. In the weaving process, each cross of the threads is interwound. In reality, there are two threads moving as one because of this interlock. It is good for the half-cross stitch (no longer recommended as a basic stitch) or any decorative stitch in which the movement is solely vertical or horizontal. If you do horizontal and vertical stitches on plain mono, every other stitch will slip because of the over-and-under nature of the weave. Doing perfect basketweave on interlocking canvas is a very arduous task. Both plain and interlocking canvas are available in several shades of beige and in stark white.

Penelope canvas has a large following of "old-time" needlepointers. This is the beige double-weave canvas used extensively in Europe to produce all those look-alike designs that have flooded the United States over the past

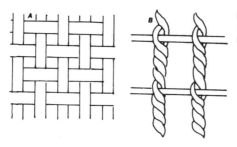

Fig. 7.2 Diagram A shows plain mono. Diagram B shows interlocking mono.

Fig. 7.3

few decades. The only point in favor of this canvas is that one can split the double threads and do both petit point and regular needlepoint on the same canvas. For instance, one could do the background and parts of the design in 10 stitches to the inch and then accent areas by doing 20 stitches to the inch. Notice the difference in stitch size in Figure 7-3.

Canvas is identified and sold by a number. The number represents the number of holes woven to the inch. No. 10 has ten holes to the inch, for example. One should be able to conclude that there are ten holes going both ways. In many instances, this is not true. If you are doing a totally geometric design, it is desirable to check the gauge before you begin. It is sometimes necessary to adjust the number of stitches so that horizontal and vertical movement will have the same width. It is most disconcerting to plan a gingham check and end up with something totally different. On some canvas, it can mean an adjustment of as much as two rows, or two stitches.

Nos. 10, 12, and 14 mesh are the most popular sizes used today. No. 10 mesh is the best for a beginner. It is not possible to achieve much detail on this size; however, you can do truly lovely things on this mesh. If a large project is planned, you will find coverage on no. 10 very rapid. No. 12 mesh is excellent when partial detail is desired, however, some beginners have difficulty obtaining good coverage on this mesh. This is because most yarns must be split to be used on this size mesh. Occasionally you will find thick and thin sections on a strand of yarn. It is always best to cut out any noticeably thin areas of individual strands. No. 14 mesh is excellent for detailed designs because the stitches are dense and smooth. It is not recommended for a first project.

No. 13 mesh is produced strictly for doing the popular Florentine embroidery work. It is obtainable in both beige and white. Yarn would normally be worked two-ply on this mesh, but when you are doing Bargello, three-ply yarn is suggested.

The smallest mesh sold today is 24/48 penelope. This is terribly small and only for the most advanced stitcher. A person's eyes must be extremely good or a magnifying glass must be used. Mono canvas is obtainable as small as no. 40 mesh, but it is not stocked in too many shops.

The most popular size mesh for detail work sold today is no. 18. It is possible to obtain trememdous detail with beautiful shading on this size, yet it normally does not cause eye strain. Yarn is used one-ply (refer to the section on yarn, page 101).

When buying canvas, check for noticeable flaws. It is not wise to needle-point over large knots. While it is possible to buy flawed canvas at a lower price, be sure to cut around the flaws. If by some chance you do find a knot in the middle of a design, be sure to touch a small drop of white glue to the rear side of the knot to keep the threads from giving way.

Sizing is very important to a project. The very smooth starchy feel of the Zweigart canvas leads to a smooth project with the least amount of yarn fray. A very rough canvas tends to fray the yarn and is very hard on your hands. All canvas (except 'soft' canvas) is stiff when it is purchased, but the stiffness soon disappears. The more you handle the canvas, the faster the sizing disappears. Soft canvas (without sizing) is used for clothing and handbags.

While smoothness of stitch does not entirely depend on the canvas, it is an integral part of your project. Soft canvas is normally found in petit point mesh size.

In the Figure 7-4 are the six most popular sizes of canvas mesh and their recommended needles. These needle sizes are merely a guide to help each individual person select the needle that is most comfortable in his or her hand. The following chart may also help guide selection:

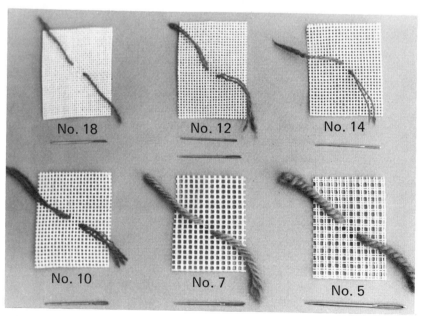

No. 18   No. 12   No. 14

No. 10   No. 7   No. 5

Fig. 7.4

no. 5 canvas	no. 13 or no. 14 needle	5-ply yarn
no. 7 canvas	no. 14 or no. 16 needle	4-or 5-ply yarn
no. 10 canvas	no. 18 needle	3-ply yarn
no. 12 canvas	no. 20 needle	2-ply yarn
no. 14 canvas	no. 22 needle	2-ply yarn
no. 18 canvas	no. 24 needle	1- or 2-ply yarn

Only the most adaptable canvas and needle sizes have been listed above. There are several other sizes available but they are not readily stocked in shops.

DO'S

Know the differences among the kinds of canvas.
Buy the right canvas for the project planned.
Buy the best quality canvas you feel you can afford.
Know before you start what effect you wish to achieve.
As a beginner, have your sketch with you when you purchase canvas.
Ask the advice of your specialty needlepoint shop.

DON'TS

Don't buy the cheapest canvas unless necessary for financial reasons.
Don't buy canvas with flaws in the wrong places.
Don't attempt too complex a first project.
Don't become discouraged if a first project is not successful.

SELECTING THE CORRECT CANVAS

The most satisfactory way for you to select the correct canvas if you are a beginner is to take a rough sketch of your design to your local shop to get some advice. If this is not possible, then hold your sketch under different types of mesh yourself. You must have a canvas with a sufficient number of holes to permit the best opportunity to follow the design.

Remember that doing round objects in a design is very difficult. It is virtually impossible to do *small* round objects on no. 10 canvas. It is much easier on no. 14. Doing round objects on a large project is much easier and for this no. 10 is satisfactory.

The color of the yarns to be used is an important criterion in deciding the correct color for your canvas. If you are using earth tones and are slightly worried about good coverage, it makes good sense to use beige canvas. If you are planning a white or very light background, under no circumstances should you use a beige canvas. Your white yarn will take on a beige cast and it will appear discolored.

If you are planning to use a dark background yarn and do not wish to paint the entire background area, you should avoid using no. 12 or no. 18

canvas. On these two sizes it is desirable to work on a painted background because of the less than perfect yarn coverage. If you do not paint the background, you might have tiny white specks showing through the dark yarn. Do not select a canvas that will cause you any eye strain. If you are unable to stitch with a thimble, it would be best to avoid anything smaller than no. 12 because the smaller needles can cause a very sore finger.

Decide very carefully: the choice of canvas is critical to the success of your project.

Fig. 7.5 Contemporary approach to design is executed in this pillow design entitled "Lovebird." Designed by Mayo. Stitched by Phyllis Keller.

Fig. 7.6 Symmetrical Imari design by Inge Woolley, Creative Needle.

YARNS

There are several brands of yarn sold that are made expressly for use in needlepoint. All are made of firmly twisted fibers. They are especially made to withstand the strain of pulling through the often rough mesh. While knitting worsteds are the correct size for no. 7 canvas, they have serious drawbacks. They tend to fray, ball, and untwist very quickly. It is far better to use them in knitting projects.

The acknowledged king of Persian yarns is manufactured by Paternayan Brothers, Inc. of New York. This brand is now carried in virtually every area of the United States. If by some chance you cannot locate it in your area, you can order it by mail from most large needlepoint stores. The fibers are lustrous and springy and seem to grow more lovely with time and wear. The color range is excellent and includes both vibrant and subdued tones.

France produces two very good yarns called Bon Pasteur and Laine Colbert. Neither of these yarns separates easily but the latter works well without separation on two-ply canvas. These yarns are not readily obtainable, but the persistent stitcher should be able to locate them. Tapestry yarn is a good, solid, three-ply yarn, but its uses are limited. For the most part, its colors are not vibrant and it is almost impossible to separate.

Another excellent yarn is called Nantucket Twist. This is a four-ply twisted yarn that works well on both no. 12 and no. 14 canvas. It also separates easily to make a two-ply suitable for no. 18 canvas. You will quickly get a feel for the various weights and will soon form strong likes and dislikes.

Paternayan also makes crewel yarn, shag yarn, and rug yarn. Crewel yarn is made for use on material rather than on canvas, but it works quite well on the smaller meshes. Shag yarn and rug yarn are made for no. 7 and nos. 3 and 5 canvas, respectively. There are also excellent crewel yarns imported from Great Britain. Multiples of any of these yarn may be used to obtain proper coverage and unusual shadings.

Quite recently, several domestic firms have begun manufacturing ''Persian'' yarns for needlepoint. If you are considering one of these, it would be wise to test a small amount before buying any quantity.

Mercerized cotton floss and pearl cotton floss are both very effective for accent and texture. The strands are simple to work with and separate easily for use on different sizes of mesh. The full strand works well on no. 14 mesh, and three-ply works well on no. 24 mesh. The piece in color plate no. 32 was worked entirely in pearl cotton on no. 14 mesh.

Silk thread is also available; however, it is very expensive and incredibly difficult to handle. Various weights are imported from France, Switzerland, and Great Britain. The sampler pillow in Figure 8-12 was worked with silk thread on no. 18 mesh. Silk thread is recommended only for the bravest of souls.

Beautiful linen thread is produced in France. It comes in a limited range of colors and does not separate easily. It works best on no. 12 mesh. It, too, is not for a beginner.

A fairly new yarn now being produced is one called acrylic Persian. If, in fact, manufacturers have been able to combine the good qualities of acrylic fibers with the good qualities of fine wool Persian yarn, then this yarn will be welcome addition to the needlepoint field.

Fig. 7.7 Decorative inset in this Aran pillow is the same stich series as seen in Fig. 2.40. Only the first six stitches were used. Difference in size results from using rug yarn #5 on canvas.

**Starting
Out Right**   Figuring yarn amounts is a very important facet of needlepoint. Every
person should know their own gauge (by this we mean the number of
stitches each strand will cover).

If you are accustomed to using one particular brand of yarn, you would
be wise to figure your gauge for at least no. 10, no. 12, no. 14, and no. 18
canvas. All you need to do to figure your gauge is to work one full strand of
yarn completely covering a one-inch width for as many rows down as the
strand will do (see Figure 7-8).

Fig. 7.8

Count the stitches and note the number on an attached tag. For instance,
no. 10 canvas contains 100 stitches to the square inch. You will be able to
work an area approximately 1 inch wide by 1½ inches long (150 stitches) for
one strand of Paternayan yarn using the continental stitch. Many stitchers
can obtain the same gauge working the more preferred basketweave stitch.
In many cases, however, the number of stitches will be slightly lower.

As you accumulate these canvas pieces, put a pin through them and keep
them in the bottom of your needlepoint bag, and you will always be prepared when buying yarn. Naturally some of this information becomes in-
grained in your mind, but if you wish to carry this information for all the
fancy stitches you will ever use, you will have to compile this data either in a
notebook or on some kind of simple chart. With this information you can
easily figure exact amounts of yarn.

Because Paternayan yarn is shipped to the various stores in a bulk state,
every store will have its own method for selling the various amounts. If, for
instance, you were going to buy from a store that sold 12 strands (approximately ½ ounce) in each skein, you would know that coverage for one full

skein would be twelve times your gauge of 150 stitches. This works out to be 18 square inches. This is approximately the area of a woman's hand slightly cupped. By moving your cupped hand over your canvas (see Figure 7-9) you can quickly figure the approximate number of skeins needed for your background. Or you may figure out the total amount needed for your design and then subtract the amount needed for your center area to give the amount needed for the background.

Fig. 7.9

If you are going to use any leftover yarn, it is especially valuable to know your exact gauge. In this way, you can figure right down to the stitch to see whether you will have enough yarn for any given area.

If you wish to build a supply of yarn, try buying accent colors by 1-ounce skeins and the more useable background colors by uncut hanks.

STORING YARN

Needlepoint yarn accumulates very quickly. Because of this, every once in a while a large project can be completed without your needing to buy any yarn, and many small projects can also be done along the way.

From the very start learn to keep your yarn neatly arranged. If you do not, it will soon be a hopeless mess. Tie small amounts of each color in small knots. Twist larger amounts as shown in Figure 7-10. It is also wise to tag your yarn with its color number and brand name.

Fig. 7.10

Although plastic bags seem like a reasonable way to keep colors organized, this is only advisable for short periods of time. Yarn needs to breathe, and the plastic will prevent this. After long periods of time sealed in plastic, the yarn will seem a bit stiff. Baskets are excellent for storage, but be sure to select those with smooth mesh so they do not snag the yarn. Baskets with lids are preferable to keep your yarns dust-free. Unfortunately, baskets require a fair amount of space.

A very practical solution for yarn storage is the use of an under-the-bed chest. They are nice and large and, most importantly, they are flat. This will permit you to see at a glance what yarn is at hand. You can use smaller shallow boxes for individual storage or separation of color. It is also wise to add breathing holes to the sides of the chest.

If you are going to buy yarn in uncut hanks, do not arbitrarily cut the whole hank in half to obtain useable lengths. It is much wiser first to roll the hank into a ball, then cut off six or seven useable lengths at a time. Many projects, such as tassels, twists, and braids, require long lengths of yarn rather than skein-length pieces.

Another thing to remember is the nap of the yarn. Yarn is produced by twisting fibers together in a long thread. Under close observation, one can see that there is a definite nap. When you double a strand in half, you are reversing the nap on one half of your yarn. For many people, this will make no difference, but some extremely advanced stitchers are very conscious of this detail. In order to check nap, slowly draw a strand through your lightly closed hand. This light pressure will either roughen or smooth the fibers. You can also hold a strand up to the light to see the nap (see Figure 7-11). If you cannot readily see the nap, then there is no point worrying about it, as it obviously will not bother you.

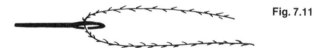

Fig. 7.11

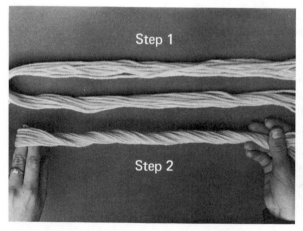

Fig. 7.12 Step I: Fold yarn in half. Step II: Twist yarn until tight.

Fig. 7.13 Bring hands together. Yarn will twist automatically. Pull cut ends through the loop.

After you have cut the proper size for your planned project, you must protect the raw edges. This can be done by any one of several methods.

The easiest way is to tape 1-inch masking tape over the edge on all four sides. Sometimes this tape will come loose during the course of your stitching. To help avoid this, apply the tape with extra pressure. The dull edge of your scissors works well for this. Simply lay the canvas on a flat surface and apply the tape with your fingers; then go back and run the dull edge of your scissors along the tape applying firm pressure. This extra little bit of effort does a great deal of good (see Figure 7-14). The big drawback to this method is that the tape will most likely fall off during the blocking process. In this case, the edges ravel rapidly. If you use tape, take extra care during the blocking process.

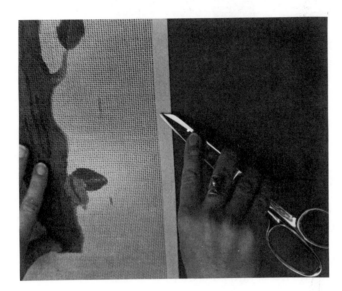

Fig. 7.14

The next best way (and, incidentally, the one preferred by many) is to turn under the edge of your raw canvas about ¼ inch and stitch it down. This can be done either with or without bias tape. If you cover the edge with bias tape, the 1-inch width works the best. You can sew it on with a simple basting stitch. If you use a machine, be sure not to use too fine a needle or too short a stitch, as both needle and thread will snap. If you are not using tape, a zig-zag stitch is preferred. This bias tape method is best for all large-scale projects because of the length of time and the amount of handling involved. When the tape is applied with stitching, it will be sure to stay attached clear through the blocking process.

The least satisfactory way is to run a small line of transparent glue around all four sides. This will definitely keep the canvas from raveling, but it leaves you with all those little sharp ends showing, and they are like a thousand hands grabbing at the yarn as you stitch.

Fig. 7.16 This three-dimensional gingerbread house was worked on #14 canvas using basketweave stitch for the four sides and turkey work (clipped) for the roof. House is approximately 18 inches square. Designed by Marge Bostwick. Executed by Judy Mackel.

HOW TO CUT ECONOMICALLY

Good canvas is expensive; but unlike normal dress fabric, there is virtually no waste at all. For tiny projects it is usually possible to buy scraps of canvas from your local store. These are usually very inexpensive. If finances permit, do not buy less than ½ yard. Allow for your finished size plus 1½ inches all the way around the article. Many experts advise 2 to 3 inches for loss, but this is excessive and can only benefit the canvas manufacturer. Figure 7-17 give a plan for a 1¼-yard purchase.

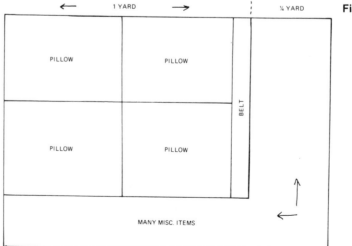

Fig. 7.17

106

From a purchase of 1 yard it is possible to get four 14 inch pillows, two belts or luggage straps, and several small projects. If you are able to buy 1¼ yards, instead of leaving a narrow 2-inch strip at the edge, you could have a very useable piece suitable for a wide variety of projects.

HOW TO HOLD YOUR CANVAS

Every expert you ask will probably tell you a different way to hold your canvas. We feel there is only one realistic way to hold a normal size canvas, and that is to roll the canvas diagonally as shown in Figure 7-18. This roll acts as a kind of stretcher bar and allows you to reach any part of the canvas without crunching the material unmercifully. This method is easy on your hands and allows the canvas to remain rigid.

With this method it is possible to finish a 14-inch pillow and still have a totally stiff canvas. The least amount of sizing loss is most desirable. DO NOT EVER CRUNCH YOUR CANVAS to reach any given area. This tends to move the individual threads and your sizing quickly disappears. The more sizing left at the end of your project, the smoother your stitches will be.

Fig. 7.18

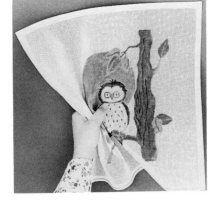

Fig. 7.19

THREADING THE NEEDLE

At first thought, one would not think it would be necessary to give detailed instructions on how to thread a needle. Threading a needle with needlepoint yarn is not like using sewing thread, however. The yarn separates very easily and this is a source of great annoyance for many a needlepointer. The technique is illustrated in Figures 7-20 to 7-22. The secret is that once you grip the yarn between your thumb and forefinger, you should not see that yarn again until it is well through the eye of the needle. Practice this until you can do it without looking. It should be an automatic motion.

This method applies only to wool yarn. If you are using silk or cotton, it is best to dampen the thread slightly and proceed as you would for sewing thread.

Remember this very important fact: YOU ARE THREADING THE NEEDLE, NOT PUSHING THE NEEDLE ONTO THE THREAD.

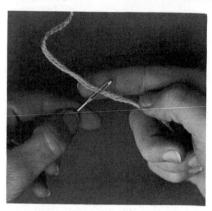

Fig. 7.20 Place yarn on forefinger with needle resting on top of yarn.

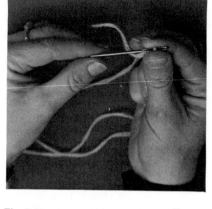

Fig. 7.21 Loop yarn around needle, pulling firmly. Pull needle out from the loop, keeping finger and thumb closed tightly on loop.

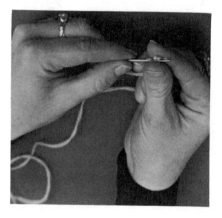

Fig. 7.22 Guide yarn through eye of needle, still keeping thumb and finger closed as tightly as possible. If you loosen your grip, yarn ply will separate and then not slip through the eye easily.

FRAME OR NO FRAME?

Many experts advocate the use of a frame. We do so only in certain instances. If you are working on fine canvas you will probably have a smoother finished product if you use a hoop or frame. By fine canvas, we mean smaller than 24 holes to the inch. If you are working on such a large piece that the very weight of it is too heavy for you to hold, then you will have to use a frame. Unless you have some physical problem with your hands or arms, there should be no other time that a frame would be necessary (see the section on pulled stitches in Chapter 9).

The biggest advantage to using a frame is that it minimizes the amount of distortion. However in most cases, it is far better to concentrate on improving your stitches and their tension than to rely on the use of a frame for this purpose. The frame is a crutch that can prevent you from ever perfecting your stitches.

The biggest disadvantage to using a frame is that you cannot take a continuous stitch; that is, you must push in the needle with one hand and pull it out from below with the other hand. This means you are making twice as many arm movements as are necessary. Using a frame not only takes away from the portability of needlepoint, but the cost of the frame must also be considered.

It *is* possible to do needlepoint that is so smooth that minimal blocking is required. Make this your goal.

RANDOM THOUGHTS

1. Strive for uniform tension. This can best be achieved by a continuous arm motion. Take a stitch and pull yarn until you reach the end. Avoid giving the yarn an extra tug as this creates a tighter tension. Above all be consistent.

2. To start a piece of yarn, begin your stitch in any given hole. Pull your yarn until about 1 inch is left hanging at the rear of the canvas. Holding this 1-inch piece with your left hand, overcast this yarn as you take your next few stitches. If you cannot manage this at first, begin by going through from the right side to the wrong side of your canvas about 1 inch from the desired first stitch hole. In the course of doing your next few stitches you will automatically catch it. Be sure to cut the thread off after you are sure that it has been secured.

3. Do not be afraid to rip out an error. It is far better to correct any error than to look at it for years to come. Ripping goes very quickly. Rip with your tapestry needle, cutting off the yarn every inch or so. Be very careful not to cut the threads of your canvas. Avoid the use of curved fingernail scissors. Do not try to "unstitch."

4. Try to keep the yarn from twisting. This will show quite badly at times. Let the yarn unwind naturally be holding the canvas upside down. It is also possible to twist your needle during the stitching process in such a way so as to counteract this twisting problem.

5. Do not attempt to use ripped-out-yarn. It will normally show as a thin area.

6. If you are going to do some intricate shading, you will find it easier to work with a short thread. Always shade from dark to light.

7. If you are going to use a two-ply canvas, decide whether you are going to use one strand doubled over or two separate ply. If you use one doubled over, begin each strand with the doubled over loop on the wrong side of your canvas and simply stitch through the loop with your first stitch. This is a wonderfully smooth way to start each strand and most economical as you save a few inches of yarn each time. It may seem like a small bit to save, but when you multiply this amount throughout the course of your project, the amount becomes quite large. Before beginning in this manner, refer back to the section in this chapter on the nap of yarn (page 104).

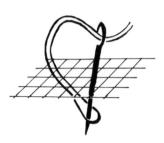

Fig. 7.23

8. If you find it difficult to follow a shape using basketweave stitch, try outlining the shape first in continental and then fill it in with basketweave. You will soon be able to eliminate this outlining step.

9. Always work in good light. Do not strain your eyes. Try very hard to use a thimble; it will be much easier on your finger.

10. Attach a pair of small scissors in some way to the handle of your needlepoint bag to avoid losing them. It is so easy to have them disappear down in the corner of a chair, and you usually discover this all too late.

11. If you are working a larger piece of needlepoint and you find that you cannot hold it in a rolled position comfortably, try hooking the roll at each end with large safety pins.

12. Try for extreme neatness on the wrong side. Do not believe someone who tells you the back side does not make any difference. Do not ever leave long threads hanging out on the wrong side. They will catch in subsequent stitches and pull through to the right side.

Fig. 7.24

13. If you find that your yarn has grown thin toward the end of the strand, cut it off. If you insist on using thin ends, you will have a lot of unplanned ridges on the surface of the work.

14. To finish off a strand, simply thread through about four stitches on the wrong side of your work, catching only the top of the yarn. Too deep a thread-through will also cause a ridge.

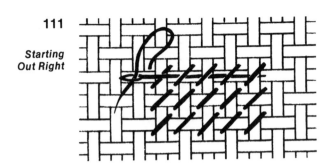

Fig. 7.25

15. Do not jump around from place to place. It is best not to jump more than four stitches. Always tunnel through the top of the stitches on the wrong side.

16. If you wish to be 100 percent economical in yarn use, keep a small plastic bag with you in which to place all your yarn ends. Not only will you not be a "litterbug," you will collect stuffing for pincushions and padding for raised areas, like that in the nose of Santa in Figure 9-87.

17. Do not select yarn from a small sample color card; inspect at least one skein of yarn. Do not select yarn in artificial light. If color is extremely important, buy one skein of yarn and try it in the light in which it will eventually be used. All light sources react differently with yarn.

18. It is wise to paint your canvas a shade close to the main color of yarn to be used. In this manner, you will avoid having any canvas peek through the yarn.

19. Do add a signature and date. This can be your own special mark, a name or just one initial. Try placing it discreetly near the edge of your design. Or, add a small frame of some special stitch with your initial inside the frame. You will not want your mark to jump out, but you will want it there.

20. Most needlepoint books are written for the right-handed person. Most left-handed stitchers can successfully read various graphs by turning the graph upside down so that the normal upper right-hand corner becomes the lower left-hand corner. If this does not work, try the graph on its side. There are now excellent books in print written specifically for the left-handed person.

21. Always keep extra needles in your bag. It is most frustrating to lose your last needle.

22. Do not keep your finished needlepoint articles on a pedestal. Walk on a rug . . . lean on a pillow. Most articles grow more beautiful with age.

23. Do not forget to allow for mounting loss when planning the size of your project. Most pillow mounters require about ¼ inch all the way around a design for loss. Some leather mounters like the same ¼ inch, and others prefer no loss at all. Upholsterers usually require a minimum of 1 inch loss all the way around.

24. If the selvage has been removed and you wish to know the original nap of the canvas, simply unravel one thread from each direction. The thread with the more pronounced bump is the straight of the canvas and

runs the same way as the missing selvage. This is valuable when you are darning holes or sewing squares together.

25. When pulling your yarn through the canvas, be sure to have your arm movement direction the same as your stitch direction. This will move your canvas threads the least amount. (Fig. 7-26).

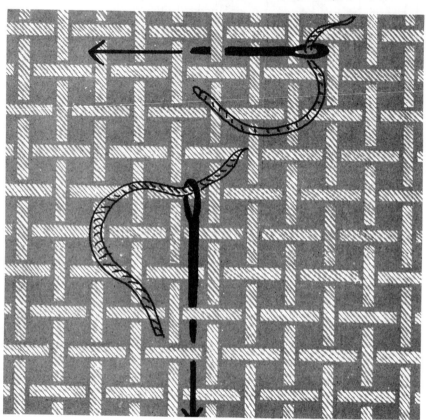

Fig. 7.26

26. If you wish to "fluff" two-ply yarn for denser coverage, rather than use a two-ply strand directly from the skein, separate the ply and then thread the needle. (Fig. 7-27)

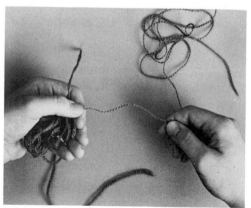

Fig. 7.27

27. Avoid starting or stopping repeatedly in the same vertical or horizontal row. Always scatter these areas. This is especially important when doing continental stitch. Stopping or starting in any concentrated area will cause a separation of stitches on the right side of your canvas.

28. When stopping or starting, always do so in a forward motion. Pulling with a backward motion can cause a slight hole on the right side of your stitching.

29. To avoid stitching in the wrong direction, always mark the top of your canvas in some manner. Simply pinning a safety pin on the top edge will solve the problem.

30. If you find that you are not going to have sufficient yarn to complete the background of your design, save out several strands of the original dye lot for blending with the new dye lot. While this will not make a join line invisible, it will minimize it greatly.

31. Avoid splitting of already worked yarn while taking a stitch. This is important both on upward and downward motions. Your needle should pierce the canvas hole, not the yarn of any preceding stitch.

32. If mending is necessary, it can be done by placing a small scrap of canvas beneath the damaged area. Make sure that the two naps are running the same direction (refer to number 24 above). Line up the holes of the two pieces and stitch through both for at least two stitches all around the hole. Carefully clip away excess to about ¼ inch on the reverse side. Run a thin line of white glue around the raw canvas edge.

33. When planning something difficult, check your design very carefully. Do not rush. It is far better to avoid complicated detail that to plan that detail incorrectly. Notice the extreme care that was taken in the planning stage of the detail shown in Figure 7-28. The pocket of the dinner jacket shown in color plate 16 is positioned with no interruption of design.

Fig. 7.28

8 To Sample or Not to Sample

Is the sampler an interesting curiosity of a bygone age? For many the mere mention of the word evokes visions of young girls bent over their stitching to master the mandatory repetoire of stitches considered prerequisite to their education.

In reality the sampler can be traced far back in the history of needlework to an age when sampling was a major form of documentation for the professional embroiderer. During the Middle Ages and Renaissance, fine embroideries were much in demand. As highly respected members of artisan guilds, each skilled craftsman developed a personal compendium of the patterns, stitches, and techniques that constituted the ''mysteries'' of the craft. Long and narrow in shape, the samplers of this period were designed to accommodate an ever-expanding vocabulary of stitches, textures, and color, and could be rolled and stored for convenient reference when not in use. In addition, this rich reference library provided testimony of the artisan's mastery in his or her craft for prospective patrons, and at the same time it

Fig. 8.1 Needlework constituted an important part of every young girl's education from the 17th century through the middle middle of the 19th century. Print from a German picture book. Courtesy of the Victoria and Albert Museum, London.

Fig. 8.2 The earliest known dated sampler has a linen ground worked in silk, metal threads, pearls, and beads in an orderly arrangement of decorative motifs. English: Jane Bostoc, 1598. Courtesy of the Victoria and Albert Museum, London.

served as a model for apprentices and amateur needleworkers for whom pattern books were nonexistent.

During the 15th and 16th centuries needlework became a major preoccupation in Renaissance households. Nobility and commoner, professional and amateur alike devoted endless hours to the pursuit of the needle in order to produce the overwhelming number of items demanded by large estates and an ornate mode of dress. No one was idle, and plying the needle gave both practical and ornamental results for an era possessed by a passion for decorating everything in sight. The sampler was an ideal tool for cataloging needlework and recording patterns and stitches destined to be shared, exchanged, and passed on from generation to generation. Samplers were in fact considered to be so valuable that they were willed to heirs and meticulously itemized in royal inventories.

The remarkable standard of excellence achieved by amateur needleworkers was still very much in evidence in 17th century samplers. Their glowing surfaces display a wealth of intricate patterns and exploratory stitching worked in silks, wools, and flax, often in combination with accents of metallic threads. The investigative nature of the sampler is retained in these 17th century examples, but their composition is more formalized and is marked by an emphasis on border patterns and letters.

It was during this period that the sampler was numbered among those precious possessions carried to the New World by the early New England colonists. These early samplers aided in perpetuating the traditional needlework patterns and techniques. Sampling in Colonial America not only provided a pleasant and sociable pastime among the village women, but it also constituted an immediate (and often the only) available source of design and pattern at a time when printed books and patterns were scarce.

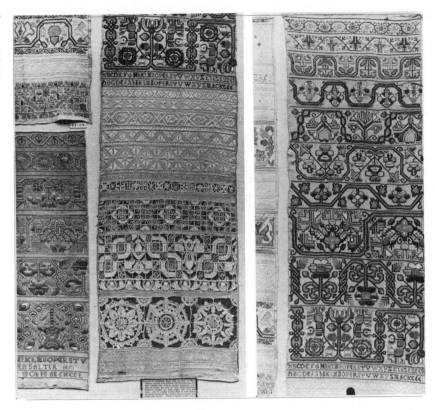

Fig. 8.3 Samplers from the second half of the 17th century
often display a number of complex motifs executed to
emphasize technical perfection and achievement in needlework.
English: Elizabeth Mackett, 1696. Courtesy of the Victoria
and Albert Museum, London.

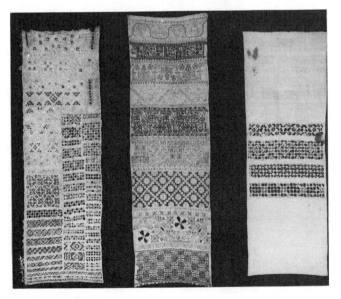

Fig. 8.4 White work sampler, white
linen tabby embroidered with
linen thread in cut and drawn work.
French knots, needle lace fillings, and
double hem stitching. England,
second half of the 17th century.
Courtesy of Royal Ontario Museum,
Toronto.

Fig. 8.5 Alphabet sampler worked by Mary Wiggin in 1797. American. Courtesy of the Philadelphia Museum of Art: The Whitman Sampler Collection: Given by Pet Incorporated.

Eighteenth-century samplers show a definitive transition in shape, function, and composition. The narrow oblong was replaced by a square or rectangular shape. The primary function of the surface no longer was used to house a fascinating accumulation of motifs and stitches, but rather the sampler became a device for display and technical virtuosity. Carefully planned pictoral compositions evolved, that were centered around biblical themes, landscapes, stylized buildings, sentimental verses, and commemorative family memorabilia. All were appropriately framed with elaborately developed embroidered borders.

Fig. 8.6 19th-century American sampler titled "Adam and Eve and the Tree of Life." Courtesy of the Philadelphia Museum of Art: The Whitman Sampler Collection: Given by Pet Incorporated.

Fig. 8.7 Embroidered sampler by Abby Bishop, American, 1796. Silk on linen. Gift of Mrs. Samuel Cabot. Courtesy of the Museum of Fine Arts, Boston.

The once highly esteemed art-craft then began to deteriorate into a mediocre handicraft. By 1870 the sampler was relegated to a disciplined exercise rather than a creative exploration. Stitches and patterns were painstakingly copied under strict supervision effectively limiting the exciting variety of textures and stitches that had once been the hallmarks of sampling. Samplers and needlework became exhibitionistic status symbols of the 19th-century "lady." Fortunately, amid the turbulence of the industrial revolution scientific advancement and industrial technology contributed a distinctive note to the creative aspects of the Victorian sampler. Aniline dyes introduced the impact of brilliance and new color into needlepoint yarns. Late in the 1800's multishaded Partridge wools appeared and provided the opportunity for needlepointers to achieve handsome gradations of color and shading with a minimum of effort and skill.

Archeological excavations at the turn of the century renewed an interest in the simplicity and elegance of the geometric motif, so masterfully incorporated in the architecture and artifacts of antiquity. Striking examples of this Victorian geometric work present a veritable feast for the eyes in marked contrast to the profusion of black-grounded posies so commonly associated with Victoriana.

After this last exuberant outburst the fate of the sampler seemed most surely consigned to oblivion. Tedium, repetitious design motifs, and the rigid restrictions imposed on technique offered little incentive to penetrate the essence of sampling.

Fig. 8.8 This 19th-century woolwork sampler displays a beautiful collection of Victorian geometric motifs executed with the consummate skill of an expert needlewoman. Courtesy of the Victoria and Albert Museum, London.

What message does the sampler hold for the 20th century craftsman? A study of its diverse surfaces will indeed give us a vivid picture of other times and other places. Within the vast range of sampling, priceless examples of folk art, tradition, and creative expression linger to inspire and motivate those who have come after. But there is yet another facet inherent in the complex structure of the sampler. The sampler signals a challenge to find new dimensions in an old technique. Canvas, needle, and yarns can only find new life through knowledge, skill, and creative endeavor. When viewed as a testing ground, the sampler beckons us to assess our skills and venture forth into new avenues of creative exploration. Its ground can tolerate error and invites familiarity with the unique qualities of its materials and stitches, which add immeasurably to the decorative impact of needlepoint design.

The exciting dimensions of sampling have no beginning and no end. In an applied art, printed words and printed patterns are seldom adequate substitutes for experience. Sampling can provide a lasting record of where you have been and a practical guide for future direction. In an art-craft that can easily become both time-consuming and expensive, sampling offers each individual an opportunity to penetrate the boundless limits of imagination in the shortest possible time at minimum expense.

Fig. 8.9 The fascinating array of stitches making up this sampler by Professor Lois Rhinesperger has been transformed into a decorative bell-pull.

Fig. 8.10 Pulled yarn worked in silk on soft #18 canvas.
Designed and worked by Ginny Ross.

When designing a rug such as this, it is easiest to begin in the center and work out. Your first sketch should be done on graph paper of like size. Painting an intricate design that must be totally counted should be attempted only by the most patient! Designed by Ginny Ross.

The Creative Potential of Needlework:
9 A Compendium

This compendium of stitches is designed as a working dictionary. It does not contain every stitch ever used. Use your own imagination to experiment and invent. Try looping, crossing over and under, backstitching, going long, going short. Establish a pattern, then repeat.

The stitch diagrams in this chapter will give you an excellent working base from which to expand. Each stitch diagram shows a series of numbers or letters. All odd numbers are considered "up" thrusts with the needle; all even numbers are considered "down" thrusts with the needle. The letters are for emphasis. The stitches are divided into basic stitches, slanting stitches, straight stitches, cross stitches, and looped stitches.

As a rule of thumb, stitches that move solely in a vertical or horizontal direction will require a slightly heavier yarn ply than regular needlepoint. For instance, Hungarian stitch worked on no. 14 canvas would need a three-ply yarn rather than the usual two-ply yarn.

All stitches have a *count*. This refers to the number of canvas threads that will be covered. It does not refer to the canvas mesh, where there are two holes for every thread. By using the count, you can easily figure the overall size of any design.

1. Basketweave
2. Basketweave Reverse
3. Continental
4. Florentine Embroidery
   a. Bargello
   b. Flame Stitch
   c. Hungarian Point
5. Half-Cross
   a. Half-Cross Trame
   b. Half-Cross Tapestry Trame
6. Smyrna Cross Stitch

CROSS STITCH

1. St. Andrews Cross
   Three-Stitch Cross
2. St. George Cross
3. Long Arm Cross
4. Rice Stitch

PULLED STITCHES

1. Algerian Eye (Star)—Double Bar
2. Diamond Eye
3. Double Pull
4. Frame (Faggot)
5. Hemstitch Variation

SLANTED STITCHES

1. Cashmere
2. Checkerboard—Chequer—Scottish
3. Fern
4. Gobelin—Encroaching—Straight—
   Slanted—Stem Stitch
5. Jacquard
6. Leaf
7. Milanese
8. Moorish
9. Mosaic (Parisian)
10. Plaid—diagonal
11. Plaid—plain
12. Web

STRAIGHT STITCHES

1. Brick
2. Hungarian

LOOPED STITCHES

1. Chain
2. Half-Moon
3. Knot
4. Ribbed Wheel
5. Turkey Knot

BASKETWEAVE

The most valuable of all stitches is the one known as basketweave. It is also probably the most confusing stitch to understand fully. Many needle-pointers can execute this stitch adequately, but few fully understand the theory of its composition. This stitch has many advantages. It supplies a firm, dense base and causes minimum distortion. There is no agony in constantly rotating your canvas; the edges are always crisp and straight.

The disadvantages are few. One is that you cannot outline with this stitch unless you are using at least a two-stitch outline. Some people also use substantially more amounts of yarn with this stitch than with other basic stitches. This problem, however, can be almost eliminated with even tension.

Fig. 9.1 Mr. Santa Claus designed and stitched by Clarie Cosgrove, aged 14. Various stitches were used, including reverse basketweave on the jacket.

Our method of perfecting basketweave is based upon the basic weaving principle that, in most woven material, 50 percent of the threads move horizontally and 50 percent move vertically. Each of the threads goes over and under the adjoining threads. Study the following illustration and hold a piece of mono canvas in your hand. Notice the direction of the threads.

Fig. 9.2

There is a down grain and there is a cross grain. Basketweave is really a two-row stitch. The first row progresses in a vertical (down) direction, and the second row progresses in a horizontal (cross) direction. Both rows have the same appearance from the front of the canvas but are pointed in different directions on the rear. Multiple pairs of these rows form a basket effect on the reverse side. This appearance has given the stitch its name.

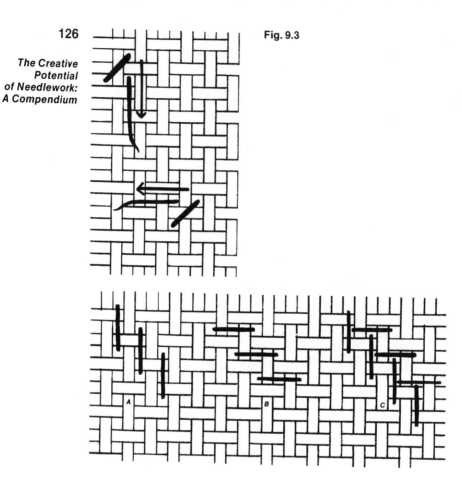

Fig. 9.3

Fig. 9.4 Diagram A shows reverse side of a vertical stitch.
Diagram B shows the reverse side of a horizontal stitch. Diagram
C shows the combination of the two stitches.

When this horizontal-vertical repeat pattern is interrupted, the reverse
side of the needlepoint will look like the diagram in Figure 9-5. Either of the
above two combinations is considered a mistake and will cause a slight ridge
on the right side of your work. Extreme care must be taken to always alter-
nate these two rows.

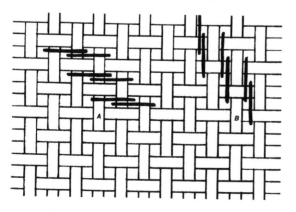

Fig. 9.5 Diagram A shows two
horizontal rows stitched together.
Diagram B shows two vertical rows
stitched together.

The stitcher must always know the direction of the next row. There are several ways to do this. One can mark the direction of the next row by carefully inserting small safety pins; or one can use small pieces of yarn tied at the correct place. One can even turn the piece over to see the reverse side every time one starts to work anew. All of these are a complete nuisance. The only foolproof method is "working on the grain." Study Figure 9-6 below. Diagram X shows the needle moving vertically and diagram Y shows the needle moving horizontally. Notice that the needle is pointing the same direction as the canvas thread that will be covered when the yarn is pulled tight. If the canvas thread is moving down, then so must your needle. If the canvas thread is moving across, then so must your needle. This is called working on the grain of the weave.

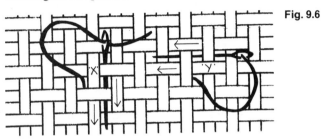

Fig. 9.6

Now is the time a try a sample. Take a piece of three-ply canvas and a needle threaded with yarn. Bring your needle up in any given hole. Study the position to decide whether you will move vertically or horizontally. Remember that the thread to study is the canvas thread that will be covered after your stitch is completed.

When you begin doing advanced designs, you will find this method invaluable. It will *always* allow you to follow intricate areas without losing track of direction. This is the only method that will guarantee flawless needlepoint. Consider the grain your built-in compass.

Turning in basketweave is also a bit confusing. First one must realize that what you are really trying to do is move down one row so that you can continue stitching. Since this is a diagonal stitch, one must advance in that direction. In Figure 9-8, a vertical row has just been completed and it is time to turn. You must place your needle in the first stitch of the next diagonal row of holes. In this case, it is hole A. In Figure 9-9, a horizontal row has just been completed. Again you must place your needle in the first stitch of the next diagonal row of holes. In this case, your needle would belong in hole B.

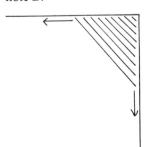

Fig. 9.7

Turning as described in Figures 9-8 and 9-9 refers only to when your edges are completely straight as in the outside perimeter of your canvas. Turning while following around a design motif can only be accomplished by "working on the grain."

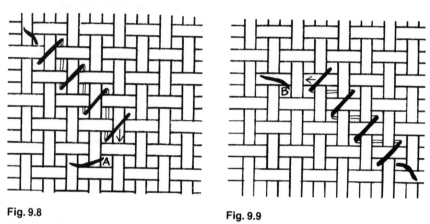

Fig. 9.8   Fig. 9.9

Stitch progression is also very important in basketweave. If you were going to begin the background of the design in Figure 9-10, you would begin at point A. You would work as far as imaginary line B, continuing down around the flower to imaginary line C. Proceed into area D. Restart at tip of the leaf working to imaginary line E. At this point, it is important that you end at point F on a horizontal row. This will permit you to make a join row of one complete row of stitches. This is the smoothest type of join row.

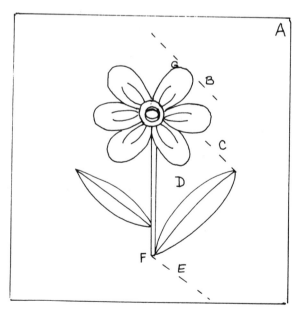

Fig. 9.10

Now go back to point G where you will restart on a horizontal row. Proceed around the left side of the flower. Work into the stem area as you did on the right side of the design, eventually arriving at point F, where you will effect a smooth, one-row join.

If you were not able to work on the grain, there would have been the possibility of several mistake areas. It is most important to check occasionally to see if you are still stitching on the grain.

One must have canvas and needle in hand to understand this stitch. Actually take a stitch. Study what we have described. This method is completely foolproof. Once you have mastered this method, needlepoint will be a joy forever!

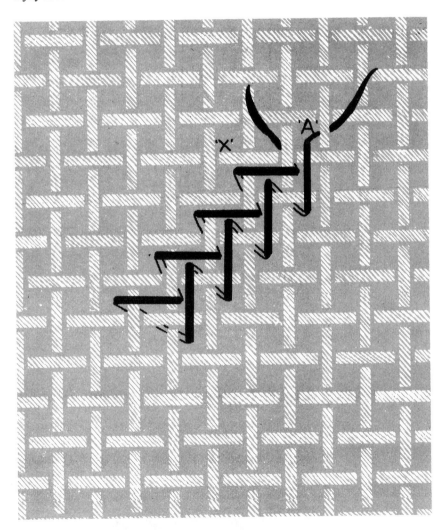

Fig. 9.11 Basketweave, reverse side. Begin at point A working down. Turn as indicated and work up. To begin new row, move to point X. Small compensation stitches must be taken to fill in between X and A.

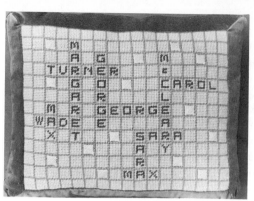

Fig. 9.12 Family tree worked as a scrabble board. Division lines were done in continental. Squares were filled in with basket weave and checkerboard. Stitched by Carol Turner.

Fig. 9.13 Continental stitch. This is an excellent basic stitch. Its biggest disadvantage is that it causes a fair amount of distortion. Diagram A shows stitch direction. Diagrams B and C show two turns. Diagram D shows how to stitch down and Diagram E shows how to stitch up. Diagram F shows the combination of two rows worked in opposing direction giving a chevron effect.

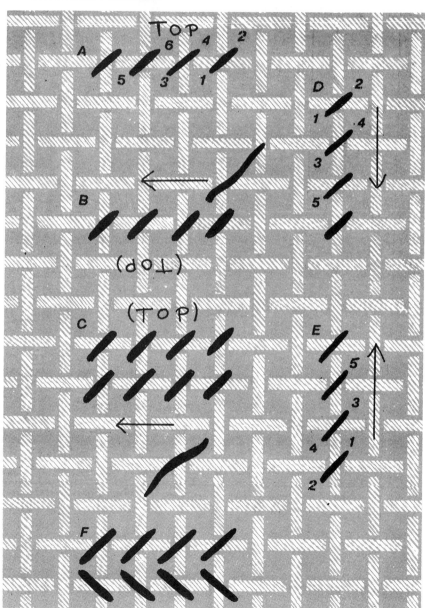

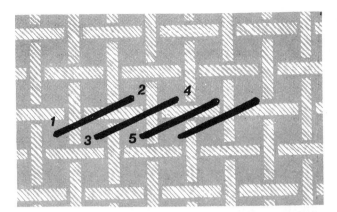

Fig. 9.15

FLORENTINE EMBROIDERY

Florentine embroidery is a broad term encompassing the three styles known as Bargello, Flame Stitch, and Hungarian Point. The three styles all use even-count vertical stitches, differing only in length of stitch and pattern direction. Various combinations of long and short stitches can achieve numerous different moods.

Flame stitch is characterized by a very pointed look accomplished by a sharp rise and fall of the stitches. While Hungarian Point has a definite rise and fall pattern, it is not as severe as Flame stitch (see Figures 9-16 and 9-17).

131

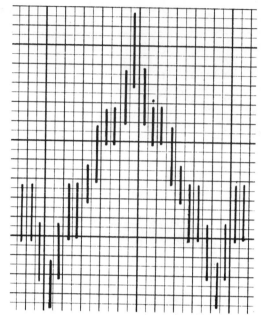

Fig. 9.16

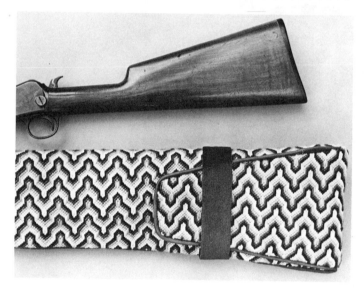

Fig. 9.17 This rifle case was worked in Hungarian point by Joan Heffner.

Bargello is the broadest group and includes limitless variations. The stitches can rise and fall or establish all-over repeat patterns (see Figures 9-18 through 9-22).

Unless a graph is used to establish your pattern, it is best to begin in the center of your canvas, working in either direction. When doing these stitches, it is necessary to use a slightly heavy yarn ply for any given canvas. For instance, no. 18 canvas would generally need one-ply yarn. When doing Bargello on no. 18, you would need two-ply yarn. To avoid canvas specks from showing through your finished work with this stitch, paint the canvas fairly close to the color of the yarn you will be using.

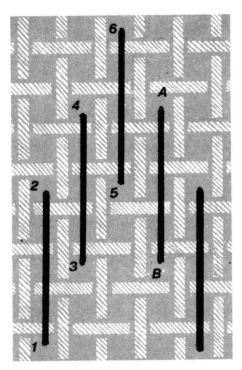

Fig. 9.18 If you wish to turn your canvas at each change of direction, you would turn between 6 and A. If you do not wish to turn, it is necessary to take a long stitch on the reverse side from 6 to B when stitching in that direction.

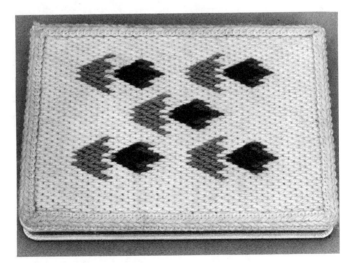

Fig. 9.19 Florentine embroidery has been applied to the top of this address book by gluing. The raw edge was covered by yarn braid.

Fig. 9.20 Regular bargello stitched in a lattice pattern using two-ply yarn on # 18 canvas.

Fig. 9.21 Random bargello is used to cover the background of this seashell design executed by Nina.

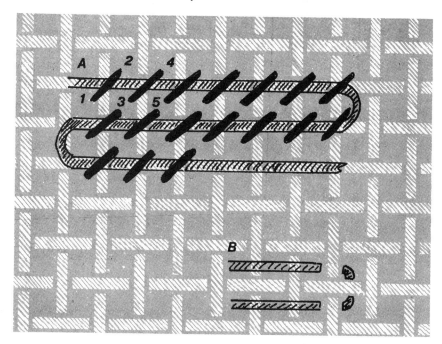

Fig. 9.22 Half cross trame. Diagram A shows tapestry trame with emphasis on yarn change as you might see in a woven tapestry. Diagram B shows plain trame with the trame thread taken to the reverse side of the canvas for the row change. Half cross (with or without trame) is most suitable for use on interlocking mono or penelope canvas.

134

Fig. 9.23 Navajo 75. This brilliantly colored rug (3′ × 5′) was worked in tapestry trame and turkey work stitch. Alternating bands vibrate with texture and pattern. Colors are pink, fuchsia, chartreuse, vanilla and light blue. Designed and stitched by Ginny Ross.

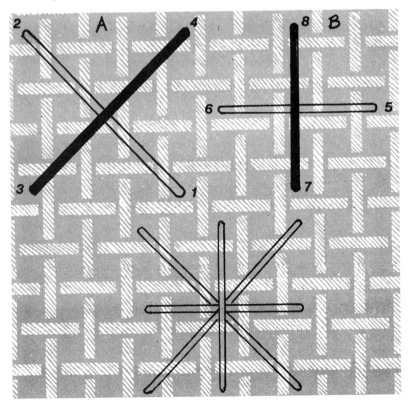

Fig. 9.24 Smyrna cross stitch. This is an excellent rug stitch when used on a geometric design. It consists of two cross stitches, one on top of the other. It can be taken over four or two threads.

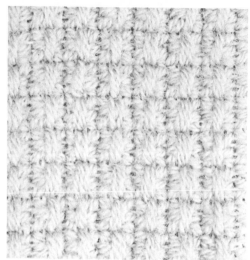

Fig. 9.25   Smyrna cross.

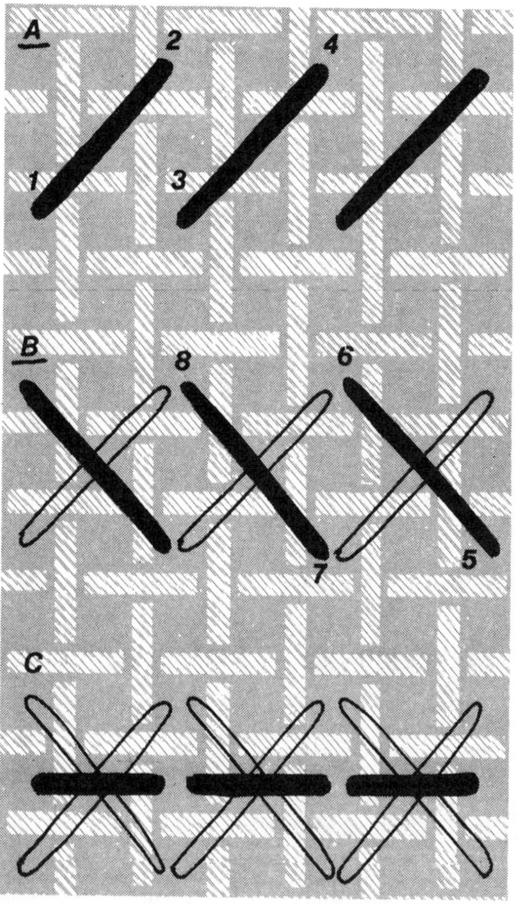

Fig. 9.27

Fig. 9.28

Fig. 9.26   St. Andrew's cross. This is a two-step stitch. Row A is followed by Row B. If step C is added, it becomes a three-stitch cross.

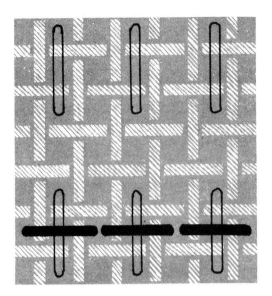

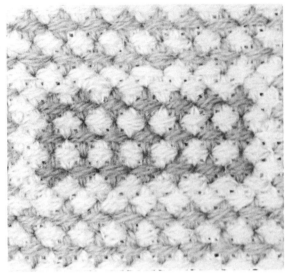

Fig. 9.29 St. George cross. This is a two-step stitch. Row A is followed by Row B. It is also possible to do each motif as a unit before proceeding to the next cross. The combination of the two crosses results in smyrna cross (see Fig. 9.26.)

Fig. 9.30

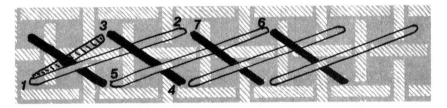

Fig. 9.31 Long-arm cross. To begin this stitch, it is necessary to take a regular compensating cross stitch. All following stitches are taken forward over four threads and back two, then forward two threads and back two threads. Illustration shows stitch used to emphasize division of pattern.

Fig. 9.32

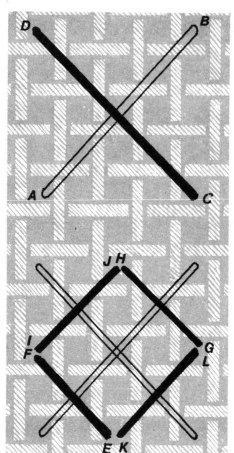

Fig. 9.33 Rice. This stitch is a series of crosses. One large cross is covered by four small crosses. The stitch can be done by first taking all large crosses, followed by many small ones. It can also be done as single units in the alphabetical order listed. This is very effective worked in two colors.

Fig. 9.34

PULLED YARN WORK

Pulled yarn work with needle-hole emphasis is centuries old. It is found in historical remnants from many civilizations. Very few 20th-century needle-pointers have utilized this medium. Many stitches you have perhaps already learned can be converted into pulled yarn work. Included in this chapter are five relatively simple stitches.

Pulled work can be used in combination with straight needlepoint and embroidery work as shown in illustration Figure 9-42. You can paint your canvas a dark color and use light yarn as shown in Figure 9-38. You can reverse the principal of dark and light as shown in Figure 9-40. You can accent background areas as shown in Figure 9-40. new 9.36

Pulled work can be done on any size canvas, but seems to be most effective on no. 14 and no. 18. The greatest amount of pull can be achieved on so-called "soft" canvas. Do not attempt to do pulled work on interlocking mono or penelope canvas. Some soft canvas necessitates the use of a frame. Use a yarn weight slightly lighter than that you would normally use on any given canvas. For instance, pulled work on no. 14 canvas would be done in one-ply wool. Linen and cotton work extremely well. Silk is more difficult to use but works well on soft no. 18 canvas (see Figure 8-10, page 121).

Strive for two important things. Be sure that your needle holes are of uniform size; and equally important, be sure your needle goes in the correct direction on the rear of your work so that the cross-over thread does not show.

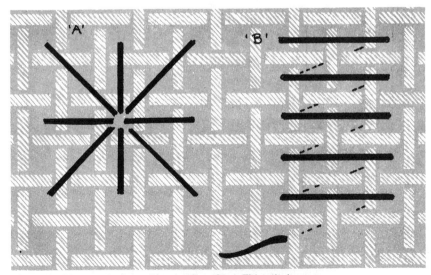

Fig. 9.35 Diagram A shows Algerian Eye (Star). This stitch may be scaled larger. All stitches originate in the center hole. Make sure that your transfer thread does not show from the right side of your work. Diagram B shows doubler of Double Bar stitch. Length and width of this stitch can be adjusted to many multiples.

139

Fig. 9.36 Double bars combine with Algerian Eye to form the decorative border of this dainty pillow. Designed by Ginny Ross. Stitched by Terry Carver.

Fig. 9.37 Diamond eye. Eye may be done as a single unit or combined for ease of stitch. All stitches go down through the center hole.

Fig. 9.38 The entire background on this pillow was first painted a dark color. Diamond eye was worked in white yarn one ply on #14 canvas. Stitched by Margaret Tullgren.

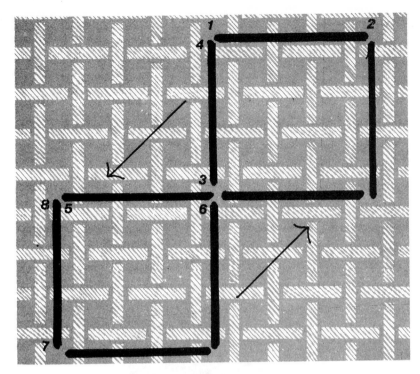

Fig. 9.39 Fagot. This stitch can be scaled satisfactorily over 2, 3, 4, or 5 threads. Use of heavy ply will give a strong check appearance, while thin ply will give a very lacy effect. Reverse canvas for second row.

Fig. 9.40 This pillow features fagot border and raised flowers worked long/short stitch and French knot. Stitched by Rosemary Ward.

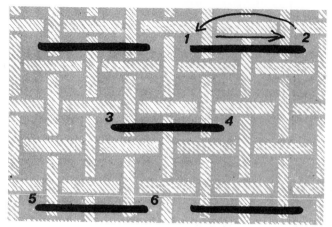

Fig. 9.41 Hemstitch variation. This is an excellent background stitch affording strong texture. It may be rescaled in many multiples. It is easiest worked in a diagonal direction. For a strong, pebbly effect, repeat pull stitch before proceeding to next stitch.

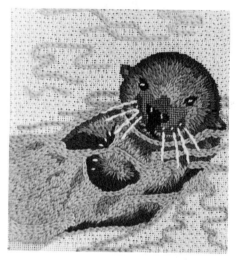

Fig. 9.42 This peaceful otter, designed by Barbara Eyre, was worked in long/short stitch. Water tracings were done in a chain stitch.

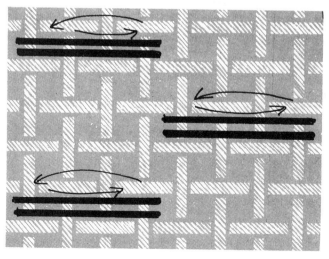

Fig. 9.43 Double pull. This stitch is excellent used as a border trim, as shown in pillow in Fig. 9.48. Notice that you are taking a double stitch over each motif. It is easiest worked in a diagonal direction.

Fig. 9.44 Pillow stitched by Mary Lue Hannah.

SLANTED STITCHES

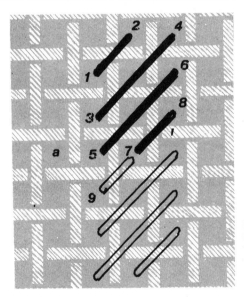

Fig. 9.45 Cashmere. This stitch can be worked vertically or diagonally from the lefthand corner. If you wish to work horizontally, begin at the right-hand side with step 7-8, 5-6, 3-4, 1-2, then to square A for next motif.

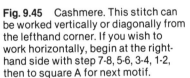

Fig. 9.46 This flower truck was de-signed by Mayo and stitched by Phyllis Keller.

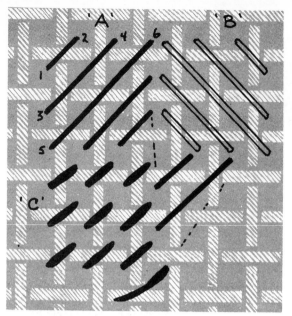

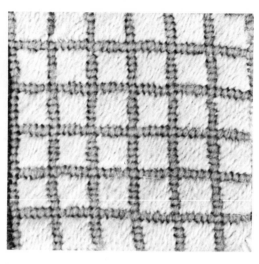

Fig. 9.47 Basic checkerboard is shown in diagram A. Work these squares diagonally. To work alternating rows (diagram B) turn your canvas so that the top is on the side (see fig. 9.76). If you wish to fill in alternating squares with basketweave, it becomes a stitch called Checquer. Basic checkerboard can also be worked without reversing direction (see Figs. 9.70 and 9.97).

Fig. 9.48 Single rows of stair-step continental can be worked first and then filled in with basic checkerboard. This becomes a stitch known as Scottish.

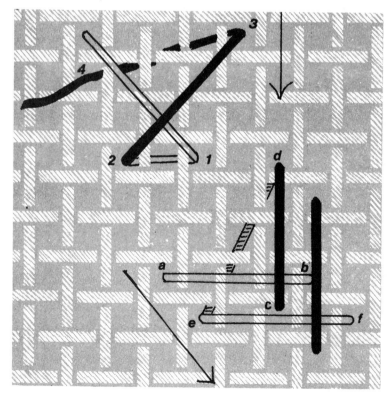

Fig. 9.49 Fern stitch can be adjusted to different lengths widths. This stitch was used in color plate 30.

Fig. 9.50   Fern stitch.

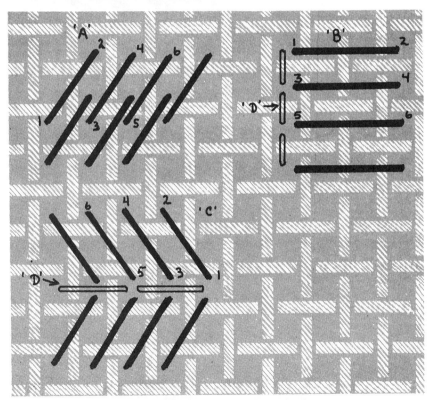

Fig. 9.51   Diagram A shows Encroaching Gobelin. Diagram B
shows Straight Gobelin. Diagram C shows Slanted Gobelin.
These three variations can be worked over many multiples of
threads to give varied effects. Diagram D shows fill-in with a
backstitch over one or two threads. The combination of C and D
is known as Stem Stitch.

The Creative Potential of Needlework: A Compendium

Fig. 9.52 This pajama pillow, designed by Barbara Simmons, was stitched by Barbara McPhee and Shirley Pool, The Elegant Stitch.

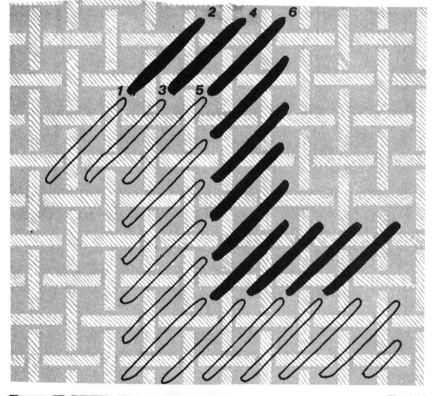

Fig. 9.53

Fig. 9.54 Jacquard. Strong stair-step quality is enhanced by the use of more than one color.

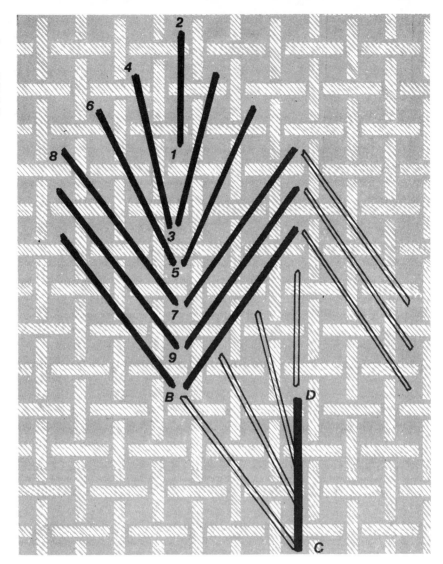

Fig. 9.55 Leaf. This is considered a difficult stitch. It can be very effective when worked in rows of different colors, such as three shades of blue. If you wish to add a stem stitch, it is done from square C to square D.

Fig. 9.56

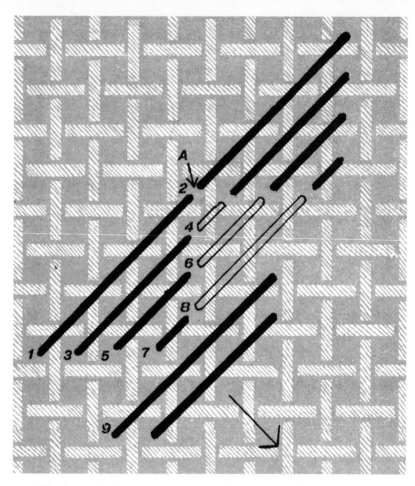

Fig. 9.57   Milanese. This stitch is worked in diagonal rows. If point A is included as a stitch on alternating rows, triangles will appear of equal size. If worked as per diagram, triangles are of different sizes. This is shown as square E in Fig. 9.97. This stitch can also be worked as shown in square N in Fig. 9.97.

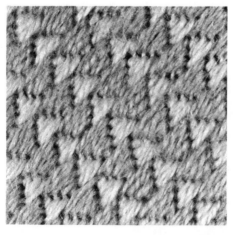

Fig. 9.58

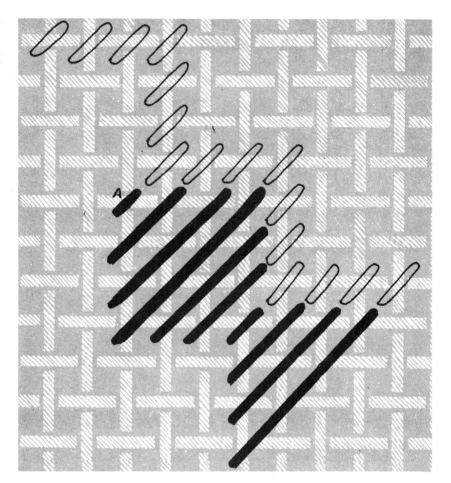

Fig. 9.59 Moorish. This stitch can be worked as diagrammed or worked eliminating stitch A, giving broader stair-step effect. It can also be worked eliminating the small stitches as shown in square M in Fig. 9.97.

Fig. 9.60

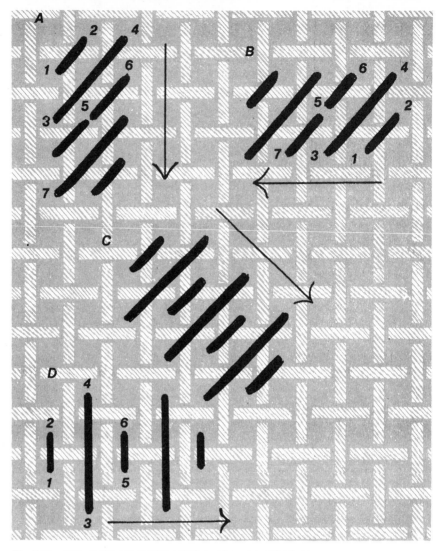

Fig. 9.61 Mosaic (Parisian). This stitch can be worked horizontally, vertically, or diagonally. If worked on the straight of the canvas, it becomes a stitch called Parisian (D).

Fig. 9.62

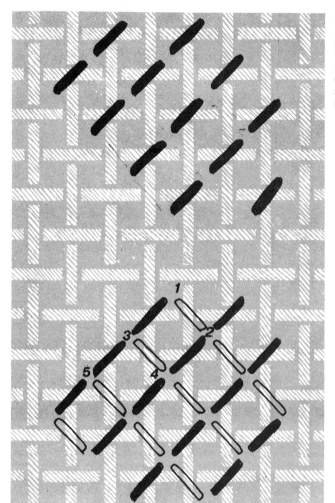

Fig. 9.63 Plaid (diagonal). When completed, this stitch gives the appearance of bias woven material. It is best worked in even numbers of rows of individual colors. First step is a series of single rows of basketweave. Second step is a row marked so that the stitch points in the opposite direction.

Fig. 9.64

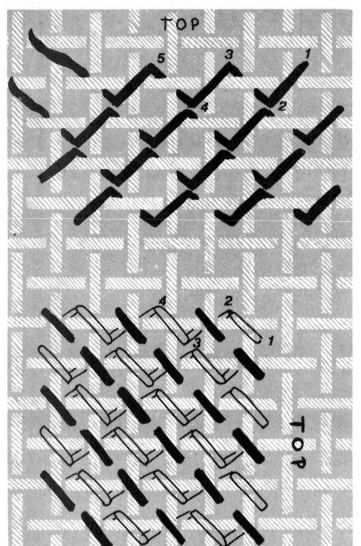

Fig. 9.65 Plaid (plain). This is a two-step stitch. Step 1 is completed for the entire canvas first. To complete step 2, the canvas is turned so that the top is at the side. This stitch should be worked in even numbers of rows. The appearance is that of woven material on the straight of the fabric.

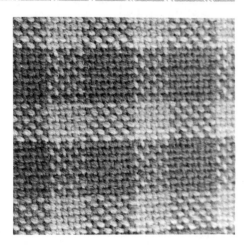

Fig. 9.66

152

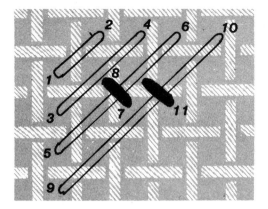

Fig. 9.67 Web. This stitch affords a strong plaited appearance. One can achieve strong directional appearance by working the stitch in opposing diagonal mesh.

Fig. 9.68

STRAIGHT STITCHES

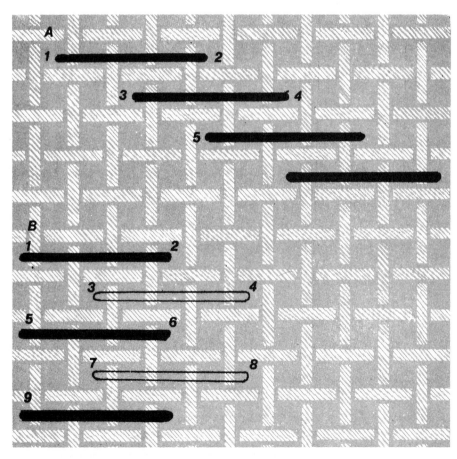

Fig. 9.69 Brick. This stitch affords very rapid coverage. It can be done over four threads and back two threads or over three threads and back two (3-2 method was used in vest shown in Fig. 2.84).

Fig. 9.70 Checkerboard. Work squares diagonally. Squares slanting in one direction are worked first. Alternating squares are worked by turning your canvas so that the top is on the side (see Fig. 9.47).

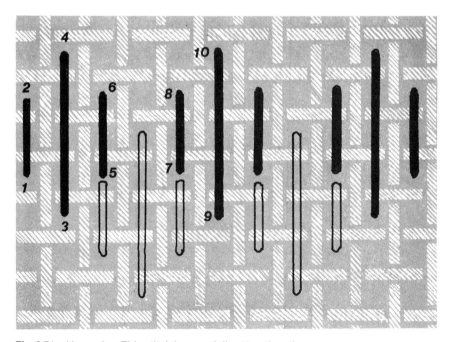

Fig. 9.71 Hungarian. This stitch is especially attractive when worked in more than one color. Notice that one complete mesh is left open between each motif. This mesh is filled in during the next row.

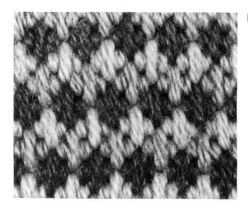

Fig. 9.72 Hungarian stitch.

LOOPED STITCHES

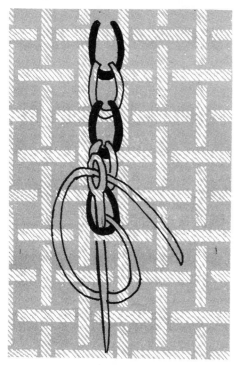

Fig. 9.73 Chain. This stitch can be re-scaled over more mesh for a longer look. It is a strong directional stitch. It was used for this purpose on the center pumpkin in Fig. 9.74.

Fig. 9.74 Design by Mayo. Stitched by Phyllis Keller.

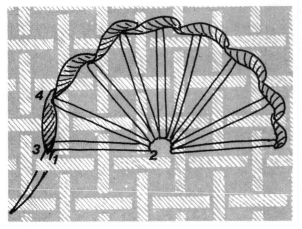 

Fig. 9.75 Half-moon. This stitch is long button-hole stitches taken through a common center hole. To square out the stitch, fill in the three stitches in each corner with basketweave stitch.

Fig. 9.76

Fig. 9.77 French knot. The yarn can be looped two, three, or four times around the needle. Be sure to take your needle up through one hole and down through another so that your knot will be locked on the surface of your work.

Fig. 9.78 The entire lamb was done in French knots. The ears were worked in turkey work. Stitched by Geri Kurek.

Fig. 9.79 Ribbed wheel. This stitch is excellent on almost any size mesh. It is used for strong decorative emphasis. Notice the small flowers in color plate, or the small single motif near the roof of the Victorian house in Fig. 2.2 Diamond design is stitched first and then looped for as many rows as desired.

Fig. 9.80

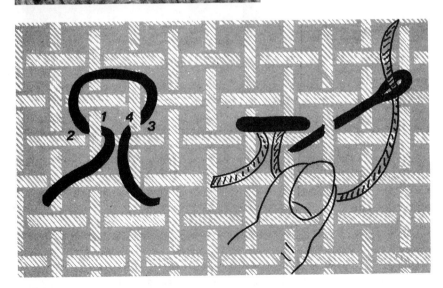

Fig. 9.81 Turkey work. This stitch can be left in a loop position or trimmed to give a fuzzy appearance. (Loop position—see Fig. 9.96; trimmed position—see pompom on Santa face in Fig. 9.87.)

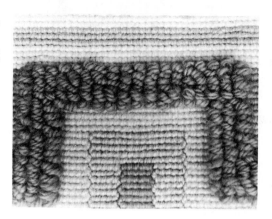

Fig. 9.82 Turkey Work stitch can be left in a loop position or trimmed to give a fuzzy appearance. (Loop position—see Fig. 9.78 or Fig. 9.23); trimmed position—see pompom on Santa face in Fig. 9.87.) Length of loop is determined by your thumb. If you have long rows of loops such as in Fig. 9.23, try looping over a pencil.

*Something Old, Something New
Something Borrowed and Something for You!*

Fig. 9.83 Handsome old Victorian chair is successfully combined with a vivid contemporary floral. Designed by Ginny Ross. Stitched by Mary Lue Hannah.

Fig. 9.84 Old twigs lashed together lend an innovative touch to a superb collection of petit point ornaments designed by Elaine Magnin.

Fig. 9.85 A new card table cover with Chinoisserie border. Stitched by Ann Seitz McBride. Designed by Ginnie Hilsinger, The Elegant Stitch.

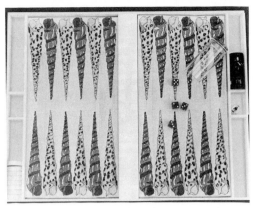

Fig. 9.86 Sea shells are expertly positioned on this backgammon board designed by Bettie Bearden, Papillon.

STUMP WORK

Stump work is the term given to raised areas on needlepoint, such as the nose on Santa Claus in Figure 9-9.87. A separate piece of needlepoint was stitched and then applied to the larger piece. Stuffing can be lambswool, cotton, or yarn scraps (see number 16 of "Random Thoughts," Chapter 7).

Plan for the separate piece of canvas to be a few stitches larger than the area to which it will be applied. Stitch the small canvas, then carefully rip out the extra canvas threads up to the very edge of the stitches. Insert all the loose ends down through the holes in the large canvas and secure them on the wrong side. Stuffing is done just before the last loose threads are secured in place. Stuffing can be inserted with either a large tapestry needle or a knitting needle.

Fig. 9.87 Santa door decoration combines crewel long-short stitch (on beard), bargelo (on hat), star stitch (cap trim), turkey work (pompom), stump work (nose), and plain basketweave. Designed by Ginny Ross and stitched by Happy Oettinger.

159

Borrow A Shape!

Fig. 9.88 A new dimension was added to this doorstep. Butterfly was separately stitched and then attached. Designed by Ginny Ross. Stitched by Geri Kurek.

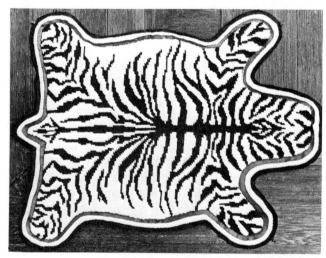

Fig. 9.89 Design borrowed from the zebra makes a striking rug. Ginny Ross.

Something For You!

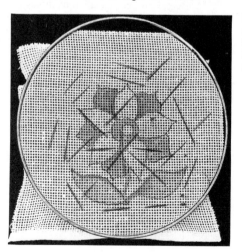

Fig. 9.90 To needlepoint any motif onto material, baste canvas securely to the cloth. Using hoop, stitch through both pieces. When finished, carefully pull out all canvas threads.

Fig. 9.91 Magnificent petit point frame designed for a treasured picture of Beverly Sills portraying Elizabeth I. Designed by Patricia Bassett Chaarte, Two Needles. Stitched by Mildred Manchester.

Fig. 9.92 This paisley design has been stitched by Mary Lue Hannah and is ready to be made into a vest. When making any kind of clothing, make sure that the overall shape is accurately measured. Many commercial patterns can be adapted to stitched garments.

Fig. 9.93 Belts are an excellent way to use leftover strips of canvas. This design by Ginny Ross was taken from a South Sea Island war shield.

Fig. 9.94 Try adding a pocket to your blazer.

Fig. 9.95 For the woman who has everything.

162

Fig. 9.96   Indian motifs were stitched on the yoke of this white wool jacket.

Fig. 9.97   Ombre strip was applied directly to the wool material of this overblouse. Five colors of wool were combined in checkerboard stitch. Any even-count loosely woven material is suitable for this type of direct stitching.

Strong stylized patchwork effectively covers the front and
back of this bolero designed by Jebba.

10 The Finishing Touch

BLOCKING

Most all needlepoint needs to be blocked before it is mounted. It is a vital step in the finishing process. A piece of needlepoint improperly blocked is most unattractive. As a rule of thumb, one can say that all needlepoint can be blocked back to its original state. There are, of course, those instances where this becomes impossible because of the tightness with which the piece was stitched, and larger pieces of needlepoint are quite difficult to stretch back into shape.

There are several ways to block needlepoint. For those that are barely distorted, a simple mild steaming on the wrong side is sufficient to allow you to pull it back into square. Use only *mild* steam, as hot steam will shrink the wool. Iron only from the wrong side. Ironing from the right side even with a protective cloth will leave a mark on the stitches. Always leave the article flat and attached in position until it is thoroughly dry and cool to the touch. *Do not take needlepoint to the cleaners.* They use steam far too hot (sometimes from the right side of your piece), and they do not have the facilities to allow for proper drying.

Most needlepoint needs to be dampened to some degree in order to pull it back into shape. In order to do wet blocking properly, you will need a wood surface that will easily accept pushpins, tacks, or staples. Some people will need a T-square in addition. Make sure that your tacks, pushpins, or staples are all nonrusting. You will also need brown wrapping paper to cover the wood surface. Large grocery store sacks opened up flat work nicely.

Although it is easier to see if your design is square when working right side up, it is far better to block right side down. The flat work surface has a tendency to straighten out slightly bumpy work. If sizing is to be applied, it is done to the wrong side of your article, eliminating the necessity of reversing your piece if you start out in that position.

If you are going to purchase a piece of wood, select a 24-inch square piece of fairly soft wood. Cover this wood with the brown wrapping paper to keep your wool from being stained by the wood. Dampen your article either by using a bottle with a mist attachment or by running your article under a slow faucet. If the piece is terribly distorted, it is advisable to let it soak for a few minutes in some cool water.

Begin by tacking or stapling the top edge of your article at about 1-inch intervals. Be sure that your tacks or staples are at least ¼ inch into the margin of unworked canvas. Using the T-square, mark the lower left- or right-hand point to which you must stretch. Begin attaching from this point across the lower edge as you did with the top edge. Now mark the opposite lower corner. Attach this corner and work to the center of the bottom edge. Now work up both sides of the article (see Figure 10-1).

Fig. 10.1

Allow the article to dry. This might take two or three days. If the article begins to buckle diagonally, sprinkle again with water. This process might have to be repeated several times. The article will eventually remain flat. When it is completely dry, take care in removing it from the board. Do not tear or jerk the article from the board. The piece might distort again or rip where the staples are. Staples are easy to remove with needle-nose pliers.

Sizing is another step in the finishing process and should be done before the article is removed from the blocking board. If you wish to size heavily to achieve a totally stiff article, the best sizing to use is rabbitskin glue. This is a powder substance obtained in art supply stores. There are full directions on the container for mixing and melting. The glue is applied in a gel state to the wrong side of the canvas.

A softer sizing can be made by mixing white glue and water. Start with equal parts glue and water and make the mixture stronger or weaker according to your preference. Brush this substance on the wrong side of your canvas. Do not saturate, as this may cause the brown paper to stick to the right side of your work. There is also now a prepared substance on the market that can be substituted for this white glue mixture. It is also possible to mix a wheat paste for this use similar to the sizing used with wallpaper.

Something that has proved very helpful recently is the use of iron-on-interfacing. This can be purchased in several weights in any yardage store. Simply cut a square and apply according to the instructions to the wrong side of your article. It is very satisfactory for bell pulls, wall hangings, and rugs. Bear in mind that the use of this interfacing seals off the wrong side of the article.

CLEANING NEEDLEPOINT

WASHING

Hand washing should be done in cool or lukewarm water. Use a mild soap and squeeze the article gently with your fingers. Do not rub or wring the needlepoint. Rinse several times. Roll in a turkish towel to remove any excess water and proceed with blocking (see page 166).

DRY CLEANING

If you take needlepoint to a dry cleaning establishment, instruct them not to use hot steam, as this will shrink the wool and the canvas. Any ironing should always be done from the reverse side. If it is painted canvas, tell them paint has been used and if any markers were used. Certain professional cleaning solvents tend to dissolve the paint and bleeding will occur. Blocking cannot be done adequately by a cleaning firm as they usually do not have facilities to attach the piece to a flat surface until it is totally dry. They will normally roll or hang the piece, making your blocking effort useless.

BLEEDING COLORS

Bleeding colors during the blocking process usually cause tragic results. If you know that the artwork is permanent and bleeding occurs, then you can assume that the yarn was not permanent. It is always wise to work on a small area if you have any doubts. In the case of bleeding yarn, quickly blot with paper towels. Do not soak or run excess water on the piece, because this will make it worse. If you go immediately to the dry cleaners and tell them the problem, they can more than likely fix the small area if it is done before it is allowed to dry. If you have knowledge that any artwork or yarn in nonpermanent, the safest thing to do is to have all the color removed by a cleaning establishment.

If the artwork runs, you can be fairly successful by holding the piece under running water until all the bleeding colors have been removed. However, it is still safer to have nonpermanent colors removed by cleaning solvents.

Spot cleaning on upholstery can be done by any of the foam cleaners. Do not ever rub needlepoint for you will make the yarn very fuzzy.

Rust and mildew can sometimes be removed by a very mild solution of hydrogen peroxide applied with an eye dropper. Be sure to neutralize the spot with plain water.

If you are going to use any of the soil preventative sprays, take care not to saturate the canvas. Ingredients in some of these products can also cause paint to bleed.

SIZING

If an unstitched piece of canvas has become quite limp, one can sometimes reactivate the sizing by a mild steaming from the wrong side. If this is unsuccessful, then try a light application of spray starch.

FINISHING EDGES

Edges can be finished in various manners. Both the bind-off stitch and straight overcast stitch are very satisfactory.

The overcast method is very effective when you wish to show a color change. This stitch can be done over as many as three or four threads. Be sure to adjust your yarn ply so that you obtain very dense coverage. The edge of your rug will always get the most wear. Basting the edge down first will make the overcast stitch easier (Figure 10-2).

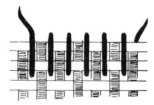 Fig. 10.2

The bind-off stitch consists of a series of figure-eight stitches worked over the edge of your canvas. Both of these stitches are excellent. It is necessary either to line your rug or to apply twill tape to cover the turned-under edge of the canvas (Figure 10-3).

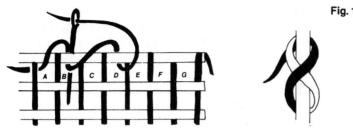

Fig. 10.3

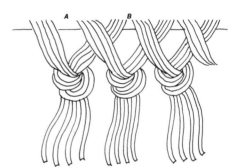

If you wish a more luxurious finish, try some hand-tied fringe. Fringe can be single knot, double knot, French braid, or a simple loop (Figures 10-4 to 10-6).

Fig. 10.4

Fig. 10.5

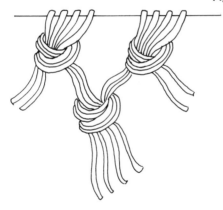

Fig. 10.6

RUG MOUNTING

Mounting a rug is not a difficult task—only time consuming. Since it is almost impossible to join pieces of needlepoint together invisibly, thought must be given during the planning process as to how best to camouflage this **169**   area.

There are three ways to minimize the seam. They are change of color, texture or design. If you do not wish to use any of these things, then you should not use a canvas mesh smaller than #8 or plan or more than one seam. If you plan a rug where there is a four corner join, you will encounter great difficulty getting the multi layers of canvas to lay flat. This can be helped by steaming and gluing before you sew the pieces together.

The easiest method of sewing the seam is to use a figure eight stitch matching row for row as you stitch. Use a linen or carpet thread. Take care that your stitch is through the canvas and not just through the yarn.

Bibliography

Today as never before we have at our disposal easy access to a wide and varied selection of beautifully illustrated books and portfolios printed both here and abroad which give extensive coverage to such topics as geometric ornamentation, historical and contemporary textiles, tapestry, tile work, Oriental rugs, mosaics, architecture, and much more. Design inspiration for needlepoint can be greatly stimulated through exposure to books of this kind.

For more specific references a select number of publications have been listed below which comprise a suggested basic needlepoint bibliography.

HISTORY

Colby, Averil. *Samplers Today and Yesterday.* The Medieval Society, 1964.

Dressman, Cecile. *Samplers for Today.* New York: Van Nostrand Reinhold Company, 1972. One of the most complete contemporary books available on sampling. It combines a well illustrated history with good basic information on design methods and inspiration.

Gostelow, Mary. *A World of Embroidery.* New York: Charles Scribner's Sons, 1975. An up-to-date historical survey including methods from Asia, Africa, South America, and Iceland. The scope covers embroidery from early civilizations to present-day movements. Many fine color illustrations supplement the text.

Grow, Judith. *Creating Historic Samplers.* Princeton: The Pyne Press, 1974. Emphasis is placed on the history and style of sampling in America with many graphs, designs, and stitches for making your own.

King, Donald. *Samplers in the Victoria and Albert Museum.* South Kensington. Large Picture Books No. 14. London: His Majesty's Stationery Office, 1960. Historical background and pictures of the collection of samplers housed in the Victoria and Albert Museum.

Symonds, Mary. *Needlework Through the Ages.* London: Hodder and Stoughton Ltd, 1928. One of the most voluminous and comprehensive volumes on needlework ever assembled and still considered a classic in the field.

TECHNIQUES

Bucher, Jo. *Creative Needlepoint.* Creative Home Library in Association with Better Homes and Gardens. Des Moines: Meredith Corporation, 1973. Good all-around information with an expanded compendium of stitches for advanced work.

Encyclopedia of Needlework. New York: Hearthside Press Inc. Publishers, 1963. A basic reference tool for all aspects of needlework. Guides to stitches, materials, and colors with full working instructions.

Frew, Hannah. *Three Dimensional Embroidery.* New York: Van Nostrand Reinhold Company, 1975. The exploration of spatial design through embroidery techniques.

Huisch, Marcus Bourne. *Samplers and Tapestry Embroideries.* London: Fine Arts Society, 1900.

Ireys, Katharine. *Finishing and Mounting Your Needlepoint Pieces.* New York: Thomas Y. Crowell Company, 1973. Covers all major details for finishing and mounting canvas work in addition to providing a resume of ideas for needlework projects.

173

Bibliography

Karasz, Mariska. *Adventures in Stitches.* New York: Funk & Wagnalls, 1949. A good collection of stitches for designers.

Mathews, Sibyl. *Modern Needlemade Rugs.* London: Mills and Boon Limited, New York: Hearthside Press, Incorporated, Publishers, 1960. Devoted exclusively to designing, stitching, and finishing needlemade rugs.

Nicholson, Joan. *Canvas Work Simplified.* New York: Arco Publishing Company Inc., 1973. An excellent beginning crafts book for prospective needlepointers with a strong contemporary design approach.

Snook, Barbara. *Needlework Stitches.* New York: Crown Publishers, Inc., 1963. General reference for stitches which range from decorative surface stitches to filling and edging stitches.

Thomas, Mary (Hedger). *Mary Thomas's Dictionary of Embroidery Stitches.* London: Hodder and Stoughton, Ltd., 1935. Comprehensive compendium of embroidery stitches for all forms of embroidery.

Index